12/5/09

· THE ·
CHILDREN'S
WORLD
ATLAS

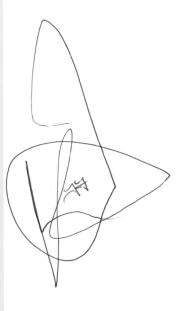

Published by
Horus Editions,
Award Publications Limited,
1st Floor, 27 Longford Street, London NW1 3DZ

First published 1991
Copyright © 1991 Ilex Publishers Limited

Second edition 1998
Third edition 2002
Copyright © Horus Editions

Text by Malcom Day, Kate Woodward and Philip Steele
Designed by Richard Rowan
Maps produced by Euromap Limited and Alan Mais
Illustrated by John Downes; Janos Marffy (Kathy Jakeman Illustration);
Chris Rothero and Clive Spong (Linden Artists)

A CIP catalogue record for this book is
available from the British Library

ISBN 1 899762 17 5

Printed in Singapore

The heading strips in this book illustrate a representative scene from each region, as follows:

Page 8 Mount Everest, Himalayas, China/Nepal; p28 Iceland; p30 Carew Castle, Wales; p32 Eiffel Tower, Paris, France; p34 Windmills, the Netherlands; p36 River Rhine, Germany; p38 Matterhorn, Switzerland; p40 Leaning Tower, Pisa, Italy; p42 Sagrada Familia, Barcelona, Spain; p44 Acropolis, Athens, Greece; p46 Budapest, Hungary; p48 St. Basil's Cathedral, Moscow, Russia; p54 Toronto, Canada; p56 New York City, USA; p60 Chichén Itzá, Mexico; p62 Caribbean beach; p66 Machu Picchu, Peru; p68 Rio de Janeiro, Brazil; p70 Atacama Desert, Chile; p76 Blue Mosque, Istanbul, Turkey; p78 Oasis, Saudi Arabia; p80 Village scene, Iran; p82 Taj Mahal, India; p84 Terraced fields, Indonesia; p86 Guilin, China; p88 Mount Fuji, Japan; p92 The Sphinx and a pyramid, Egypt; p94 Kilimanjaro, Tanzania; p96 Cape Town, South Africa; p100 The harbour, Sydney, Australia; p102 Rotorua, New Zealand; p104 Easter Island, Pacific; p106 Antarctica.

∘ THE ∘
CHILDREN'S
WORLD
ATLAS

HORUS EDITIONS

CONTENTS

HOW TO USE THIS ATLAS   5
PLANET EARTH   6
THE PHYSICAL WORLD   8
CLIMATE AND VEGETATION   10
WORLD ANIMALS   12
WORLD NATIONS   14
WORLD POPULATION   16
LANGUAGES AND RELIGIONS   18
LAND USE AND AGRICULTURE   20
MINERALS AND INDUSTRY   22

EUROPE   24
SCANDINAVIA AND FINLAND   28
BRITISH ISLES   30
FRANCE   32
BENELUX   34
GERMANY   36
AUSTRIA AND SWITZERLAND   38
ITALY   40
SPAIN AND PORTUGAL   42
SOUTH-EAST EUROPE   44
CENTRAL EUROPE   46
FORMER SOVIET UNION   48

NORTH AMERICA   52
CANADA   54
UNITED STATES OF AMERICA   56
CENTRAL AMERICA AND
   MEXICO   60
CARIBBEAN ISLANDS   62

SOUTH AMERICA   64
NORTHERN SOUTH AMERICA   66
BRAZIL   68
SOUTHERN SOUTH AMERICA   70

ASIA   72
TURKEY AND NEAR EAST   76
ARABIAN PENINSULA   78
SOUTH-WEST ASIA   80
SOUTH ASIA   82
SOUTH-EAST ASIA   84
CHINA AND KOREA   86
JAPAN   88

AFRICA   90
NORTHERN AFRICA   92
WESTERN, CENTRAL AND
   EASTERN AFRICA   94
SOUTHERN AFRICA   96

OCEANIA   98
AUSTRALIA   100
NEW ZEALAND   102
PACIFIC ISLANDS   104

ARCTIC AND ANTARCTICA   106

GENERAL INDEX   108

MAP INDEX   109

HOW TO USE THIS ATLAS

In this atlas the world is divided up into six parts: the continents of North America, South America, Europe, Asia and Africa, and the region known as Oceania which includes Australasia and the islands of the Pacific. At the beginning of each section you will find a political map showing the countries which make up each continent or region, together with facts and figures telling you about the area. population and capital of each of these countries. On the following pages, physical maps illustrate the land's surface, showing mountains, forests, deserts, ice, savanna, steppe and cultivated land.

To find out what the colours, symbols and abbreviations on the maps in this book mean, check the key on this page. If you want to look up a place, either on a map or in the text of this atlas, use the indexes at the back of the book.

Look at the location map to find out the position of a country or region in the world.

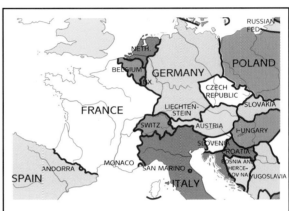

A political map shows how the world is divided into different countries.

KEY
Physical environments

Forest

Savanna/steppe/ cultivated land

Desert

Mountains

Tundra

Ice

Country border

State boundary

Ottawa ■
Capital city

Milan ●
City (population over 1 million)

Puebla ●
City (population under 1 million)

Salem □
State capital

Olympus
▲ 2917
Mountain and height in metres

Brenner Pass
Mountain pass

River

Seasonal river

Lake

Seasonal lake

Canal

A physical map shows the mountains, lakes, deserts, forests and grasslands that cover the Earth's surface.

Map abbreviations
Arch.	Archipelago	Mts.	Mountains
Aust.	Australia	Neth.	Netherlands
C.	Cape	N.Z.	New Zealand
Fr.	France	Pen.	Peninsula
I.	Island	Pk.	Peak
Is.	Islands	Port.	Portugal
L.	Lake	Pt.	Point
Mt.	Mount	Sp.	Spain

UK   United Kindom
US   United States of America

Text abbreviations
km.	kilometres
sq. km.	square kilometres
m.	metres
cm.	centimetres
ft.	feet
in.	inches

Scale
The bar scale will enable you to work out real distances between two points shown on the map. Measure the number of centimetres on the map and then compare it to the number of kilometres or miles on the bar scale.

5

PLANET EARTH

Large groups of stars, gas and dust are called galaxies, and there may be over 100 billion galaxies in the Universe. Our own galaxy is called the Milky Way, and it contains billions of stars. The Sun is just one of these stars, a tiny speck in the vastness of space.

However, if the Sun is compared with the planet Earth, it seems huge. The nine known planets of the solar system orbit this great ball of burning gas, which provides the warmth that makes life possible on Earth. Many of the planets are themselves orbited by moons. Earth has only one moon, but it has been proved that Uranus has at least fifteen, Jupiter seventeen, and Saturn at least 22. Other objects within the solar system include thousands of asteroids, tiny planets and rock fragments which orbit mainly between Mars and Jupiter.

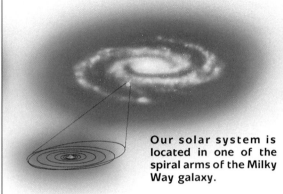

Our solar system is located in one of the spiral arms of the Milky Way galaxy.

Solar system facts

Planet	Diameter (km. (miles))		Time taken to orbit the Sun
Mercury	4878	(3100)	88 days
Venus	12,104	(7521)	224.7 days
Earth	12,740	(7916)	365.4 days
Mars	6739	(4212)	687 days
Jupiter	141,622	(88,000)	11.9 years
Saturn	114,263	(71,000)	29.5 years
Uranus	51,800	(32,116)	84 years
Neptune	49,424	(30,642)	164.8 years
Pluto	2414	(1500)	247.7 years

The inner planets

In 1976, two American Viking spacecraft landed on Mars, 79 million kilometres away from Earth. They revealed a barren, rocky landscape, with air reddened by suspended dust, but found no evidence that life ever existed there. Earth is the only planet in the solar system where life is possible. The surface of Venus, Earth's nearest neighbour, is too hot. Its poisonous clouds float in a dense atmosphere. Mercury, the nearest planet to the Sun, has a very thin atmosphere.

The solar system

Pluto

Neptune

Comet

Meteoroids

Uranus

Asteroids

Mars

Jupiter

Saturn

Venus

Sun

Earth

Mercury

The Earth: our planet

The centre of the Earth is called the core. The inner core is thought to be made up of a great ball consisting mostly of solid iron, extending about 1200 kilometres from the centre. The metals of the core are intensely hot, with a temperature of about 3700 degrees Celsius. In the outer core, a layer about 2240 kilometres thick, the metals are liquid. The whole core is surrounded by the mantle, a great layer of rock about 2900 kilometres thick. The surface of the Earth is called the crust and is a thin layer of rock. Some ocean floors rest on crust only six kilometres thick, but at its thickest, beneath the great mountain ranges, the crust is 70 kilometres deep.

The outer shell of the Earth is made up of sections called plates. The great heat from the Earth's centre makes these plates move. Normally, this happens so slowly that we do not notice it. Over millions of years the edges of some of these plates squeeze against each other, pushing up ranges of mountains. Sometimes, if a sudden movement occurs at the boundaries of the plates, an earthquake takes place. Then, the earth shakes and cracks open.

Above the land and sea, the atmosphere extends 500 kilometres into space. This layer of air is a mixture of gases which includes nitrogen, oxygen, argon, carbon dioxide and water vapour. Air, soil and water are warmed and lit by the rays of the Sun, 150 million kilometres away in space. The atmosphere screens out many other rays which might harm life on Earth.

The Earth rotates on its axis every day. The part facing the Sun is in daylight, while the other side of the Earth has night. The planet takes 365 days and six hours to orbit the Sun.

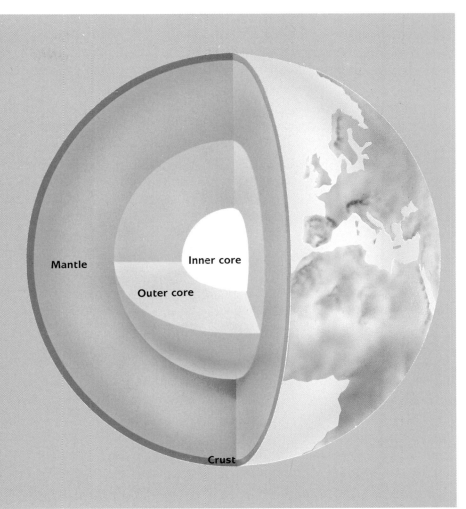

The outer planets

Some astronomers think that there may be ten planets, but only nine have been discovered so far. Each planet spins round as it orbits the Sun. Pluto, smaller than our Moon, is normally the farthest from the Sun. However, at times its orbit swings in nearer to the Sun than that of Neptune. Uranus is tilted over on its side. Saturn is famous for its beautiful rings, made up of dust and ice; they were first identified by the Dutch astronomer, Christiaan Huygens, in 1655. Jupiter is the largest planet in the solar system. It is a planet of violent storms, one of which forms a great swirling red spot that can be seen through a telescope from Earth. Both Saturn and Jupiter are covered by oceans of liquid hydrogen.

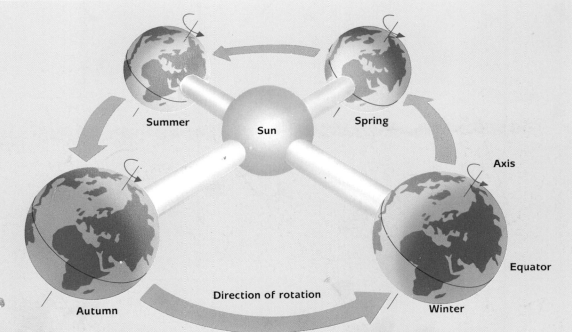

The four seasons

An axis is an imaginary line round which a planet spins. The Earth's axis is tilted at an angle from the upright. This means that as the Earth orbits through space, parts of its surface are tilted towards the Sun. In summer, when the northern hemisphere is tilted towards the Sun, it has warmer weather and longer daylight hours. Later, when it tilts away from the Sun, the season there turns to autumn. The colder, shorter days of winter are caused by the northern hemisphere being tilted at its farthest away from the Sun. Spring brings back warmth and longer days as the north starts to tilt towards the Sun again. In the tropical regions along the Equator, there is less seasonal contrast.

7

THE PHYSICAL WORLD

This physical map of the world illustrates the surface of the Earth with its mountains, plains, deserts, lakes and rivers. Over two-thirds of the Earth's surface is covered by water. There are four vast oceans, the Pacific, Atlantic, Indian and Arctic. The seas surrounding Antarctica are sometimes counted as a fifth, known as the Southern Ocean. On this map the biggest ocean, the Pacific, is split into two.

Features in *relief* stand out on the map. You will see the Himalaya mountain range which contains the highest peaks in the world, and major river systems such as the Nile in Africa and the Amazon in South America. The gold-coloured areas represent the dry expanses of deserts, such as the Sahara, the Gobi Desert in central Asia, the arid lands of the Australian interior and the driest place on Earth, the Atacama Desert in Chile.

Regions of the world	Area sq. km.	(sq. miles)	Approximate Population
North America (including Mexico and Central America)	25,349,000	(9,785,000)	477,322,000
South America	17,611,000	(6,798,000)	340,693,000
Europe (including European Russia)	10,498,000	(4,053,300)	701,031,000
Asia (including Asian Russia)	45,066,000	(17,400,000)	3,620,132,000
Africa	30,335,000	(11,709,000)	779,041,000
Oceania	8,923,000	(3,444,278)	30,194,000
Antarctica	13,340,000	(5,149,240)	none permanent

Earth Facts
Distance round the Equator 40,074km. (24,902 miles)
Distance round the Poles 40,008km. (24,860 miles)
Distance to the centre of the Earth 6370km. (3958 miles)
Average distance from the Earth to the Sun 150,000,000km. (93,210,000 miles)
Average distance from the Earth to the Moon 384,403km. (238,857 miles)
Speed at which the Earth orbits the Sun 29.8km. per second (18.5 miles per second)
Total surface area of the Earth 509,803,110 sq. km. (196,836,000 sq. miles)
Total land area of the Earth 144,485,136 sq. km. (55,786,000 sq. miles)
Total area of water on the Earth 365,318,000 sq. km. (141,050,000 sq. miles)
Coldest recorded temperature on the Earth Vostok, Antarctica (−89.2°C/−128.6°F)
Hottest recorded temperature on the Earth San Luis, Mexico (57.8°C/136°F)
Place on the Earth with highest average rainfall Mount Waialeale, Hawaii (average annual rainfall 1168cm./460in.)
Driest place on the Earth Atacama Desert, Chile (no rain from 1570–1971)

Largest Lakes

	sq. km.	Area (sq. miles)
Caspian Sea (Asia)	372,000	(143,630)
Superior (Canada/USA)	82,348	(31,795)
Victoria (Africa)	69,484	(26,828)
Aral (Asia)	68,682	(26,511)
Huron (Canada/USA)	60,700	(23,430)
Michigan (USA)	58,020	(22,395)
Tanganyika (Africa)	32,900	(13,860)

Largest Deserts

	sq. km.	Area (sq. miles)
Sahara (northern Africa)	9,000,000	(3,475,000)
Australian	1,554,000	(600,000)
Arabian	1,295,000	(500,000)
Gobi (central Asia)	1,295,000	(500,000)
Kalahari (southern Africa)	583,000	(225,000)

Highest Waterfalls

	Drop m.	(ft.)
Angel Falls (Venezuela)	979	(3212)
Tugela Falls (South Africa)	947	(3110)
Utigard Falls (Norway)	800	(2625)

Largest Islands

	sq. km.	Area (sq. miles)
Greenland	2,175,601	(840,004)
New Guinea	800,510	(312,085)
Borneo	757,050	(292,000)
Madagascar	587,041	(226,658)
Sumatra	524,100	(202,300)
Baffin Island	476,065	(183,810)
Great Britain	229,870	(88,730)
Honshu	227,999	(88,031)

Longest Rivers

	Length km.	(miles)
Nile (Africa)	6671	(4145)
Amazon (South America)	6515	(4050)
Yangtze (China)	6300	(3915)
Mississippi-Missouri-Red Rock (North America)	6212	(3860)
Ob-Irtysh (Russia, Kazakhstan)	5570	(3460)
Yenisei (Russia)	5539	(3442)
Huang (Yellow River) (China)	5464	(3395)
Congo (Africa)	4700	(2920)
Amur (Russia)	4416	(2744)
Lena (Russia)	4400	(2735)
Mackenzie-Peace (Canada)	4240	(2635)

Oceans

	Area sq. km.	(sq. miles)	Greatest depth m.	(ft.)
Pacific	165,240,000	(63,800,000)	11,033	(36,198)
Atlantic	82,439,355	(31,830,000)	9216	(30,238)
Indian	74,850,690	(28,900,000)	7725	(25,344)
Arctic	14,245,000	(5,500,000)	5500	(18,050)

Highest Mountains

	Range	Height m.	(ft.)
Mount Everest	Himalayas (China/Nepal)	8848	(29,028)
K2 (Godwin Austen)	Karakoram (China/India)	8611	(28,250)
Kanchenjunga	Himalayas (India/Nepal)	8586	(28,170)
Makalu 1	Himalayas (Nepal/China)	8463	(27,766)
Cho Oyu	Himalayas (Nepal/China)	8201	(26,906)
Dhaulagiri	Himalayas (Nepal)	8167	(26,795)
Manaslu	Himalayas (Nepal)	8163	(26,781)
Nanga Parbat	Himalayas (India)	8126	(26,660)

ARCTIC OCEAN

Lena

Ob

Siberia

Amur

EUROPE

Volga

Alps

Danube

Gobi

ASIA

Indus

Himalayas

Yangtze

Ganges

Sahara

Niger

Nile

AFRICA

Congo

PACIFIC OCEAN

INDIAN OCEAN

AUSTRALIA

SOUTHERN OCEAN

CLIMATE AND VEGETATION

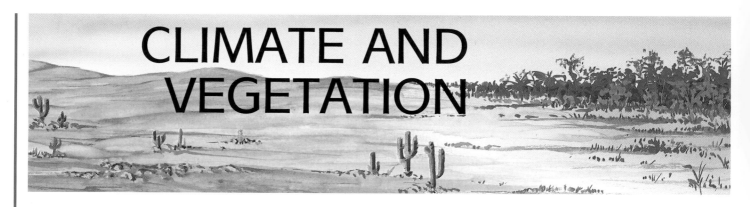

The pattern of weather recorded at any one place over a long period is called the climate. The climate in Greenland, near the North Pole, is bitterly cold. The climate in equatorial Zaïre is warm and moist, or humid. The climate of a region is affected by its location on the planet, by its height above sea level, by its proximity to oceans or mountains, and by local winds. Different plants and animals are suited to different climates.

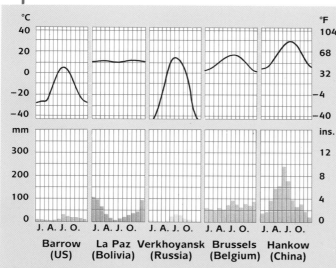

Barrow (US)   La Paz (Bolivia)   Verkhoyansk (Russia)   Brussels (Belgium)   Hankow (China)

For each climate station, the upper graph gives the average monthly temperature, the lower graph the average monthly rainfall. The colour of the rainfall bars corresponds to the climatic zone in which the station is located, shown on the map.

Singapore   Williston (US)   Adelaide (Australia)   Minna (Nigeria)   Bahrain

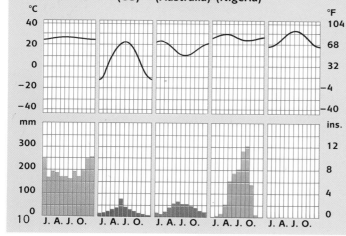

Barrow

Williston

La Paz

The world's biomes

A climatic zone which is home to certain kinds of creatures and plants is called a biome. The graphs on the left show the rainfall and temerature range of ten different biomes. These are marked on the map on the right.

1 Tundra Treeless plain, frozen for much of the year, covered in grasses, mosses and low plants.

2 Mountain Dwarf shrubs and alpine plants provide low cover above the treeline.

3 Taiga Evergreen trees and shrubs which keep their leaves all the year round.

4 Temperate deciduous forest A milder climate produces trees which shed their leaves in autumn, such as oak and beech.

5 Temperate rainforest A mild, rainy climate favours ferns, mosses and tall trees.

6 Tropical rainforest A warm, humid climate produces a dense tangle of vegetation and trees.

7 Temperate grassland Rolling grassy plains, prairies, or steppes, cover much of central Asia now, and at one time much of the United States and Canada.

8 Scrub Open bush country with thorn, shrubs or grassland.

9 Savanna The burning hot plains of central Africa are covered in coarse grasses and scattered trees.

10 Desert Sand and rock with little water. Home to tough plants such as cacti.

Temperature and rainfall

Water from the world's lakes and oceans evaporates, or turns into vapour. This rises into the air, and cools to form drops which fall as rain or snow. The world's pattern of winds is caused by the differences in temperature between the Poles and the Tropics.

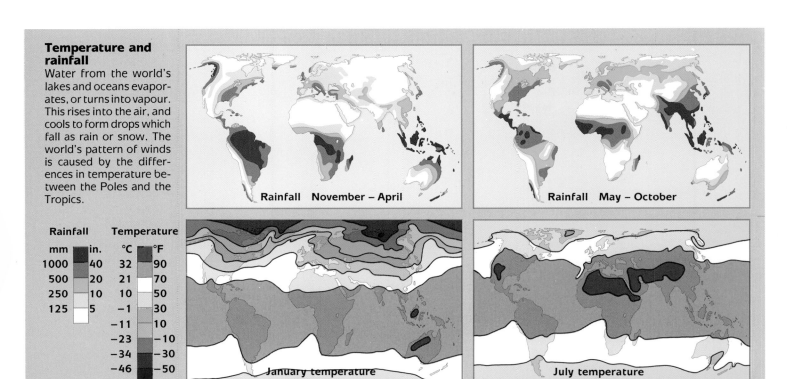

Rainfall   November – April

Rainfall   May – October

Rainfall		Temperature	
mm	in.	°C	°F
1000	40	32	90
500	20	21	70
250	10	10	50
125	5	−1	30
		−11	10
		−23	−10
		−34	−30
		−46	−50

January temperature

July temperature

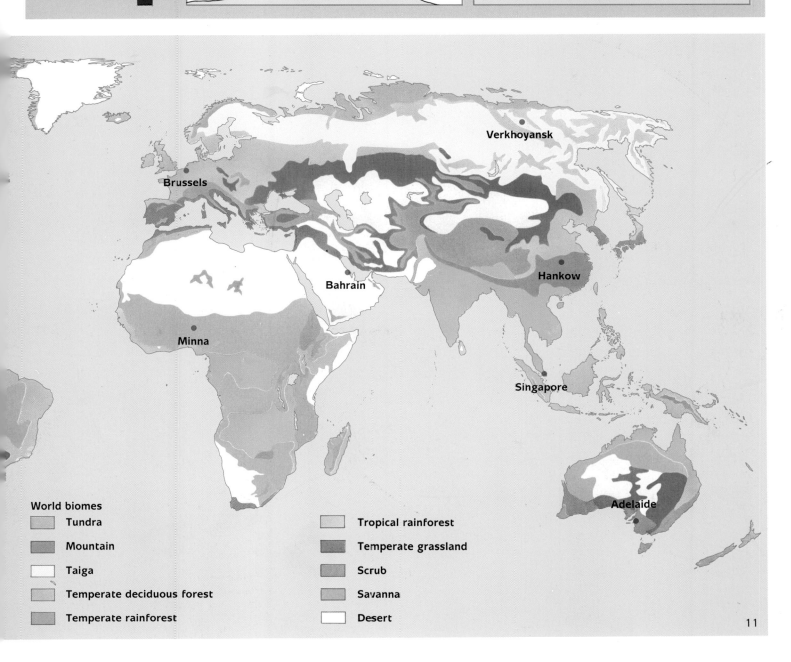

World biomes

- Tundra
- Mountain
- Taiga
- Temperate deciduous forest
- Temperate rainforest
- Tropical rainforest
- Temperate grassland
- Scrub
- Savanna
- Desert

11

WORLD ANIMALS

Over millions of years many different kinds, or species, of creatures have developed on Earth, from the great whales of the oceans to the elephants of the African plains. Insects are the most numerous creatures on Earth. Humans are the most intelligent species, but their activities now threaten the survival of the world's wildlife.

Sea otter

The world's animals

The 4230 species of mammal include whales, lions and tigers, monkeys and humans. There are more than 8000 bird species, most of which can fly. Unlike birds and mammals, reptiles cannot control their own body temperature. There are more than 5000 species including snakes, lizards, crocodiles and turtles. The 2500 amphibians include frogs, toads and newts. Fish number over 30,000 species.

All these creatures have bodies supported by skeletons. They are far outnumbered by invertebrates, or spineless animals. These include insects, worms, spiders, crabs and shellfish.

The world's oceans

The blue whale is the largest animal on Earth. It feeds on small shrimps called krill. The seas support a great wealth of animal life, including mammals such as the whales and dolphins, thousands of species of fish, seabirds, seals and sea lions, squid, octopus, sponges, corals and jellyfish.

Marine iguana

South America

The huge wings of the Andean condor help it to soar high above the South American peaks. The mountains are also inhabited by llamas and alpacas, members of the camel family, used for carrying goods and shorn for their wool. Monkeys, parrots and giant snakes live deep in the rainforests of the Amazon.

North America

The American Arctic is home to polar bears and seals. The great forests of Canada and Alaska are inhabited by moose, the largest deer in the world. The grasslands or prairies were once roamed by vast herds of bison (also called buffalo). Some have survived despite being hunted to the verge of extinction in the nineteenth century.

Arctic tern

Harp Seal

Moose

Chipmunk

Beaver

Prairie dog

Elf owl

Monarch butterfly

Manatee

Roadrunner

Condor

Armadillo

Torrent duck

Toucan

Giant anteater

Vicuna

Amazon river dolphin

Blue whale

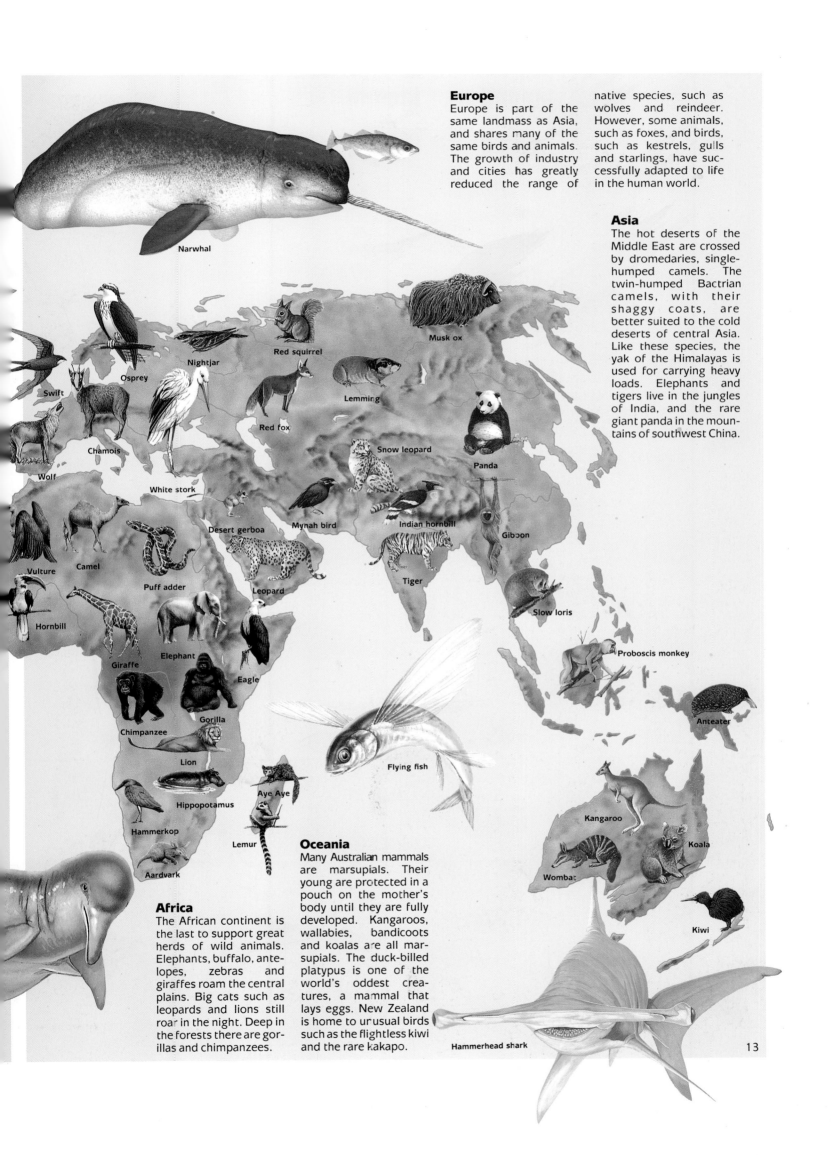

Europe
Europe is part of the same landmass as Asia, and shares many of the same birds and animals. The growth of industry and cities has greatly reduced the range of native species, such as wolves and reindeer. However, some animals, such as foxes, and birds, such as kestrels, gulls and starlings, have successfully adapted to life in the human world.

Asia
The hot deserts of the Middle East are crossed by dromedaries, single-humped camels. The twin-humped Bactrian camels, with their shaggy coats, are better suited to the cold deserts of central Asia. Like these species, the yak of the Himalayas is used for carrying heavy loads. Elephants and tigers live in the jungles of India, and the rare giant panda in the mountains of southwest China.

Africa
The African continent is the last to support great herds of wild animals. Elephants, buffalo, antelopes, zebras and giraffes roam the central plains. Big cats such as leopards and lions still roar in the night. Deep in the forests there are gorillas and chimpanzees.

Oceania
Many Australian mammals are marsupials. Their young are protected in a pouch on the mother's body until they are fully developed. Kangaroos, wallabies, bandicoots and koalas are all marsupials. The duck-billed platypus is one of the world's oddest creatures, a mammal that lays eggs. New Zealand is home to unusual birds such as the flightless kiwi and the rare kakapo.

Narwhal

Osprey
Swift
Nightjar
Chamois
Wolf
Red squirrel
Lemming
Red fox
White stork
Musk ox
Snow leopard
Panda
Camel
Vulture
Desert gerboa
Puff adder
Mynah bird
Indian hornbill
Gibbon
Hornbill
Leopard
Tiger
Slow loris
Giraffe
Elephant
Eagle
Gorilla
Chimpanzee
Lion
Hippopotamus
Aye Aye
Flying fish
Hammerkop
Lemur
Aardvark
Proboscis monkey
Anteater
Kangaroo
Koala
Wombat
Kiwi
Hammerhead shark

13

WORLD NATIONS

The world is made up of about 200 countries – an exact count is impossible because the total number varies, depending on how the term is defined. The majority are independent nations, governing themselves. The rest are either territories governed by other countries, or unions of smaller states.

Countries are organized and governed in different ways. Monarchies are ruled by kings or queens. Republics are headed by an elected president. Many countries have democratic governments, in which representatives are elected by the people. The elected representatives make up national assemblies, congresses, or parliaments.

COUNTRY FACTS

The largest countries of the world

	Area sq. km.	(Area sq. miles)
Russia	17,076,223	(6,593,391)
Canada	9,976,139	(3,851,810)
China	9,571,300	(3,695,500)
USA	9,372,570	(3,618,700)
Brazil	8,511,965	(3,286,488)
Australia	7,628,300	(2,966,151)
India	3,287,590	(1,269,350)
Argentina	2,766,889	(1,068,302)
Kazakhstan	2,714,215	(1,048,000)
Sudan	2,505,813	(967,500)

The smallest countries of the world (excluding dependencies)

	Area sq. km.	(Area sq. miles)
Vatican City	0.44	(0.17)
Monaco	1.6	(0.65)
Nauru	21.3	(8.2)
Tuvalu	24.6	(9.5)
San Marino	60.5	(23.4)
Liechtenstein	160	(62)
Marshall Islands	180	(70)
Malta	316	(122)
Grenada	345	(133)
St. Vincent & the Grenadines	388	(150)
Barbados	430	(166)
Antigua & Barbuda	442	(171)

The most populous countries of the world

	Population
China	1,231,571,000
India	997,515,000
United States	278,230,000
Indonesia	207,022,000
Brazil	167,967,000
Russia	146,195,000
Pakistan	134,790,000
Bangladesh	127,669,000
Japan	126,570,000
Nigeria	123,897,000

1 Denmark
2 Netherlands
3 Belgium
4 Luxembourg
5 Switzerland
6 Austria
7 Czech Republic
8 Slovakia
9 Hungary
10 Albania
11 Cyprus
12 Lebanon
13 Israel
14 Kuwait
15 Qatar
16 Brunei
17 Singapore
18 Togo
19 Benin
20 Equatorial Guinea
21 Rwanda
22 Burundi
23 Georgia
24 Armenia
25 Azerbaijan
26 Tajikistan
27 Moldova
28 Slovenia
29 Croatia
30 Bosnia and Hercegovina
31 Macedonia
32 Yugoslavia

The United Nations flag

United Nations

Many independent nations join together with others in order to form international groupings such as the European Union, the Caribbean Community, the League of Arab States, or the Organization of African Unity.

The largest international organization of all is made up of 186 countries. This is the United Nations Organization, founded by 50 countries in 1945. These founding members wished to ensure a peaceful future for the world.

The United Nations (UN) has not always been able to prevent war, but it has helped to solve some of the world's problems. Member nations have sent troops in UN uniform to various trouble spots around the world.

The head of the United Nations is called the Secretary General.

Delegates from all the member nations meet each year at the General Assembly, held at the organization's headquarters in New York City.

Fifteen nations form the Security Council, which meets to discuss crises and policy. Five nations – the USA, UK, Russia, France and China – are permanent members. Each of the other ten is elected by the General Assembly for a two-year term.

Some of the most important work of the UN is carried out by its agencies. These bodies deal with working conditions, food and agriculture, world health, finance, trade, communications, education, science and culture.

15

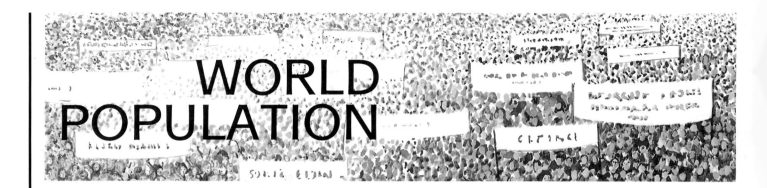

WORLD POPULATION

In most countries, a census is taken every ten years or so, from which governments can count the number of people living within their borders. Population figures are important, for they help in the planning of housing, education, health care and agriculture. Organizing a census can be very difficult in some parts of the world, where people live in remote deserts or mountains. China alone has a population of more than one billion, the world's highest.

More than 6 billion people live in the world today, and about 160 babies are born every minute of the day. Such a vast number of people needs enough food to stay alive and healthy. In the world's richer countries there is often too much food, which goes to waste. In the poorer regions of the world, food shortages and undernourishment are common.

Population Density

Parts of the planet are very heavily populated. A high birthrate and limited territory are factors in high population density. In numerous countries, many people move to cities in search of work, adding to the congested conditions. Refugees (people fleeing from war or famine in their own land) increase the populations of other countries.

The tiny principality of Monaco, on the southeast coast of France, has a population density of about 20,000 people per square kilometre. Bangladesh (about 890 people per square kilometre), Bahrain (about 960), and the Netherlands (about 410) are among the most densely populated countries. This compares with 30 per square kilometre in the United States. In contrast, some countries seem nearly empty:

Libya and Canada have about three people per square kilometre; Australia has about two; and Mongolia has less than one. Greenland has only one for every 38 square kilometres, while the continent of Antarctica has no permanent population.

The map of population density (right) shows that the world's most crowded places lie in Asia, Europe, and the eastern United States.

Major cities of the world

City	Population	City	Population
Mexico City	16,674,000	London	7,285,000
São Paulo	16,583,000	Cairo	6,955,000
Buenos Aires	14,400,000	Tehran	6,759,000
Shanghai	13,580,000	Bangkok	6,547,000
Mumbai (Bombay)	12,596,000	Lima	6,465,000
Beijing	11,300,000	Istanbul	6,407,000
Kolkata (Calcutta)	11,022,000	Bogotá	6,276,000
Seoul	10,289,000	Dhaka	6,050,000
Tianjin	9,420,000	Rio de Janeiro	5,552,000
Moscow	9,270,000	Chennai (Madras)	5,422,000
Karachi	9,269,000	Santiago	5,181,000
Jakarta	9,160,000	St. Petersburg	5,130,000
Delhi	8,419,000	Shenyang	5,120,000
Tokyo	7,854,000	Hyderabad	4,254,000
New York City	7,323,000	Bangalore	4,130,000

Population per sq. km.	per sq. miles
100	250
50	125
25	62.5
10	25
1	2.5
	Uninhabited

■ Cities with over 5 million inhabitants

• 1-5 million inhabitants

World population growth

In 1975 the population of the world was four billion. By 1999 it had grown to six billion. The map on the right shows how the population grew over that period.

Ten thousand years ago, the world population stood at about five million. By the middle of the next century, it will have reached more than eight billion. This rapid growth in population is sometimes referred to as an explosion. It has been caused by improvements in medicine and health care, in the growing of crops and the supply of food.

The rate of population growth is now slowing down, but the number of humans is still increasing by about 90 million every year.

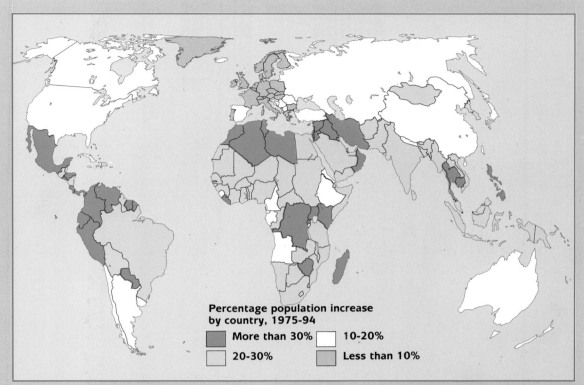

Percentage population increase by country, 1975-94

- More than 30%
- 20-30%
- 10-20%
- Less than 10%

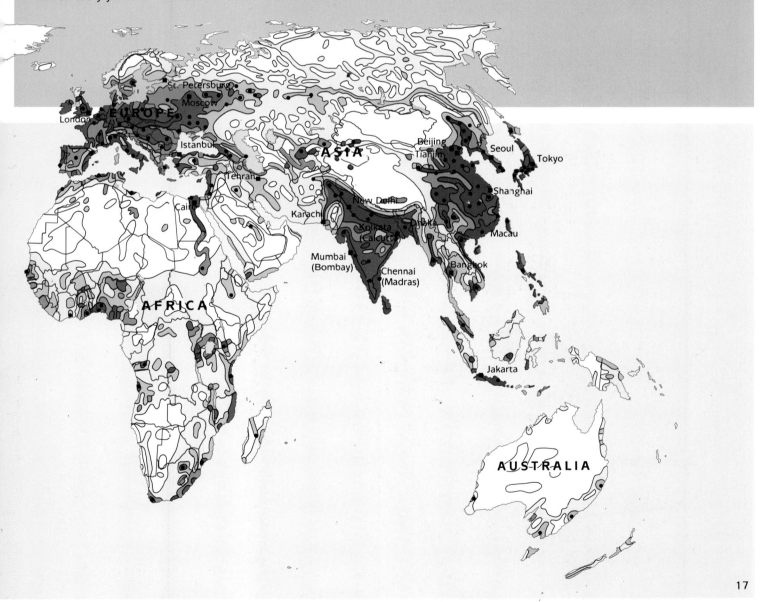

LANGUAGES AND RELIGIONS

Each continent is home to many different peoples. All share common concerns and interests, whatever the colour of their skin, or their religious or political beliefs.

The way of life followed by any one group of people is called a culture. There is a rich variety of cultures in the world today. Despite a worldwide system of communications, people have not adopted identical ways of life. They are proud of their historical backgrounds and their regional customs. There are often many different cultures within a single country; for example, 56 ethnic groups live within China alone.

About 5000 languages are spoken around the world, and they are written down in a number of different alphabets and symbols. Many languages have regional variants, or dialects.

Languages of the world

	Estimated number of speakers
Mandarin (Chinese)	999,000,000
English	487,000,000
Hindi	457,000,000
Spanish	401,000,000
Russian	280,000,000
Arabic	230,000,000
Bengali	204,000,000
Malay-Indonesian	194,000,000
Portuguese	186,000,000
Japanese	126,000,000
French	126,000,000
German	124,000.000

Religions of the world

	Estimated number of followers
Christianity	1,999,560,000
(Roman Catholic)	1,057,327,000
(Protestant)	347,408,000
(Orthodox)	215,128,000
Islam	1,188,242,000
Hinduism	811,337,000
Buddhism	359,981,000
Sikhism	23,259,000
Judaism	14,443,000
Baha'ism	7,107,000
Confucianism	6,299,000
Jainism	4,218,000
Shintoism	2,762,000
Chinese folk religions	384,807,000
Ethnic religions	228,366,000
Atheists	150,089,000

Language families

Indo-European
- Germanic
- Romance
- Slav
- Baltic
- Greek
- Albanian
- Armenian
- Iranian
- Hindi

Altaic
- Turkic
- Mongolian
- Korean

Religions and beliefs

From earliest times, humans have tried to find out the meaning of their lives and of the world around them. People have worshipped the Sun and Moon, the natural world, and all kinds of spirits, gods and goddesses. Three great faiths were born in the deserts of the Middle East: the followers of Judaism, Christianity and Islam all believe in a single God. India saw the rise of Hinduism, Buddhism and Sikhism. Taoism and Confucianism began in China, and Shinto in Japan. Atheism is the belief that there is no God.

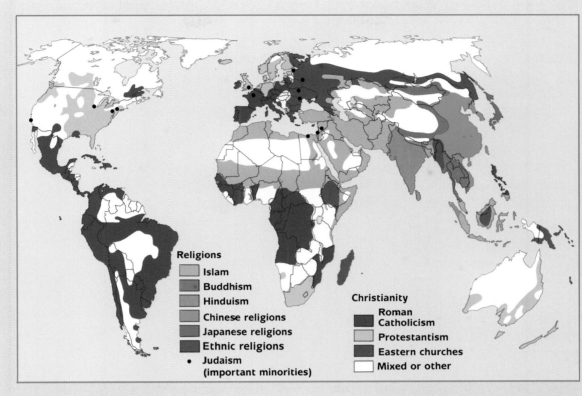

Religions
- Islam
- Buddhism
- Hinduism
- Chinese religions
- Japanese religions
- Ethnic religions
- Judaism (important minorities)

Christianity
- Roman Catholicism
- Protestantism
- Eastern churches
- Mixed or other

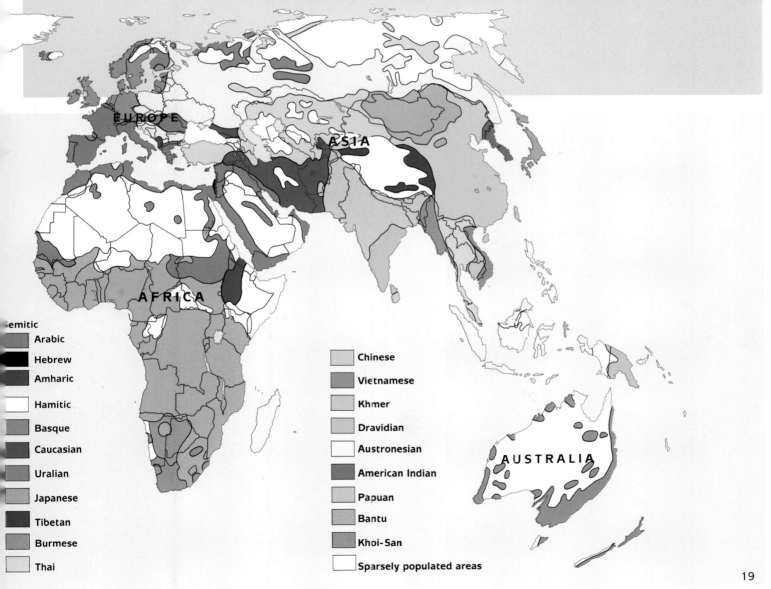

EUROPE

ASIA

AFRICA

AUSTRALIA

Semitic
- Arabic
- Hebrew
- Amharic
- Hamitic
- Basque
- Caucasian
- Uralian
- Japanese
- Tibetan
- Burmese
- Thai

- Chinese
- Vietnamese
- Khmer
- Dravidian
- Austronesian
- American Indian
- Papuan
- Bantu
- Khoi-San
- Sparsely populated areas

LAND USE AND AGRICULTURE

The first humans lived by gathering wild nuts, fruits and vegetables, by hunting, and by fishing. Ten thousand years of farming have seen the clearing of much of the world's great forests and the cultivation of former grasslands. The growing of basic foodstuffs, or staple crops, is vital to feed the world's population. Modern methods have enabled richer countries to produce more food than they need, while in poor countries the opposite is often true.

Each pie chart shows how total world production is shared between the top producers listed below.

* Commonweatlh of Independent States

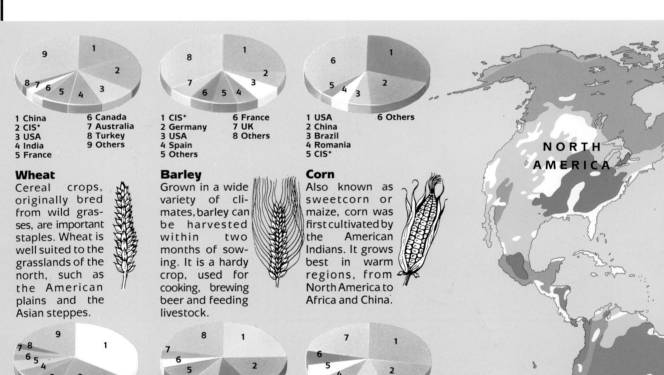

1 China
2 CIS*
3 USA
4 India
5 France
6 Canada
7 Australia
8 Turkey
9 Others

Wheat
Cereal crops, originally bred from wild grasses, are important staples. Wheat is well suited to the grasslands of the north, such as the American plains and the Asian steppes.

1 CIS*
2 Germany
3 USA
4 Spain
5 Others
6 France
7 UK
8 Others

Barley
Grown in a wide variety of climates, barley can be harvested within two months of sowing. It is a hardy crop, used for cooking, brewing beer and feeding livestock.

1 USA
2 China
3 Brazil
4 Romania
5 CIS*
6 Others

Corn
Also known as sweetcorn or maize, corn was first cultivated by the American Indians. It grows best in warm regions, from North America to Africa and China.

1 China
2 India
3 Indonesia
4 Bangladesh
5 Thailand
6 Vietnam
7 Myanmar
8 Japan
9 Others

Rice
Originally a grass grown in wet river valleys, rice is now the world's most important staple crop, feeding half the world's population. It is normally grown in warm climates.

1 USA
2 India
3 China
4 Mexico
5 Nigeria
6 Argentina
7 Sudan
8 Others

Sorghum
The sorghums are various kinds of grass, widely grown for food and cattle fodder. They form an ideal crop for regions where there is usually a long hot, dry season.

1 India
2 China
3 Nigeria
4 CIS*
5 Mali
6 Niger
7 Others

Millet
In North America millet is chiefly grown as animal food. Millet is also grown in the warmer parts of Europe, Africa and Asia, where it is an important food crop.

NORTH AMERICA

SOUTH AMERICA

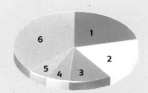

1 India   6 Indonesia
2 China   7 Others
3 Sri Lanka
4 Kenya
5 Turkey

1 Brazil   6 Ethiopia
2 Colombia   7 Uganda
3 Mexico   8 Indonesia
4 El Salvador   9 Others
5 Guatemala

1 China   6 Others
2 USA
3 India
4 Pakistan
5 Brazil

1 Italy   6 Others
2 France
3 Spain
4 Argentina
5 USA

1 Malaysia
2 Indonesia
3 Thailand
4 Others

Tea

The mountainous regions of China, India and Sri Lanka are suitable for growing tea. This tropical evergreen shrub needs a fertile soil and a warm, rainy climate. It prefers higher elevations and is grown on terraced hills.

Coffee

This small tree was first grown in Africa. It was later introduced from Arabia to Java, the Caribbean, Brazil and India. Its red berries contain two hard beans. These are roasted and ground into a powder.

Cotton

Inside the seed heads, or bolls, of the cotton shrub is a mass of white fibres up to five centimetres long. These are cleaned and untangled, spun into yarn and woven into cloth. Cotton is grown in many warm lands around the world.

Grapes

Vines are grown for their grapes, which are eaten fresh or dried to make raisins. Many are pressed, and the juice is fermented, a process which turns the grape sugar into alcohol. Grape vines are grown on sunny hillsides.

Rubber

The commercial or Pará rubber tree is a native of Brazil which was later introduced to south-east Asia. When the trunk is cut, a milky white gum oozes out to protect the tree. This substance, called latex, is processed to make rubber.

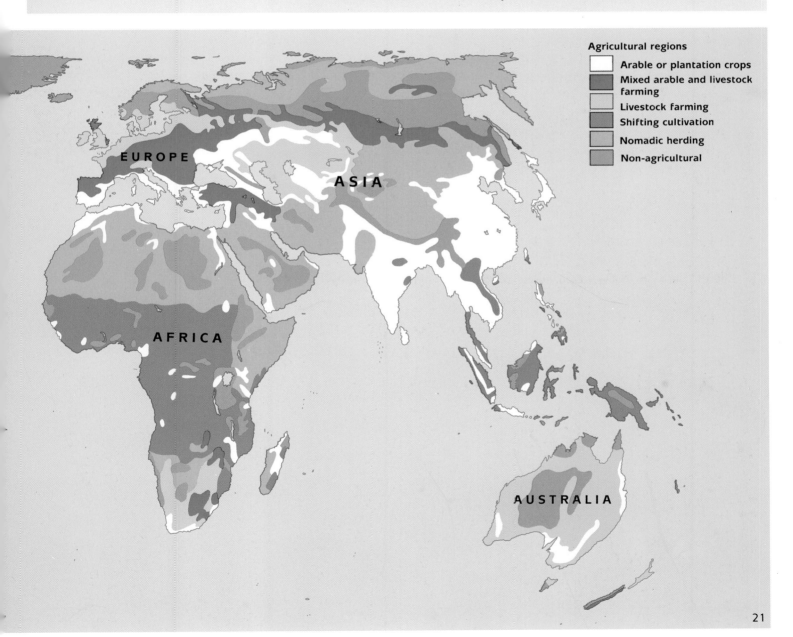

Agricultural regions

- Arable or plantation crops
- Mixed arable and livestock farming
- Livestock farming
- Shifting cultivation
- Nomadic herding
- Non-agricultural

EUROPE

ASIA

AFRICA

AUSTRALIA

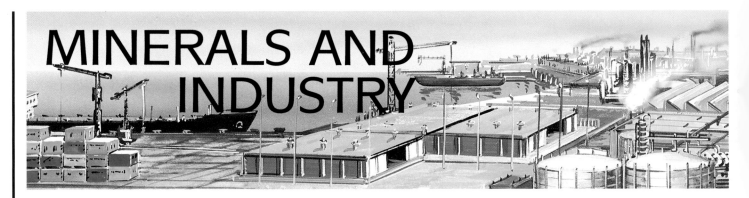

MINERALS AND INDUSTRY

Beneath the surface of the Earth lies a wealth of minerals. These include ores, or rocks which contain metals, and fuels such as coal, oil or natural gas. Manufacturing industries use energy and raw materials to produce goods. Countries rich in these natural resources can build up their manufacturing industries, or increase their wealth by selling the minerals to other countries. Countries lacking in natural resources must import them.

Each pie chart shows how total world production is shared between the top producers listed below.
*Commonwealth of Independent States

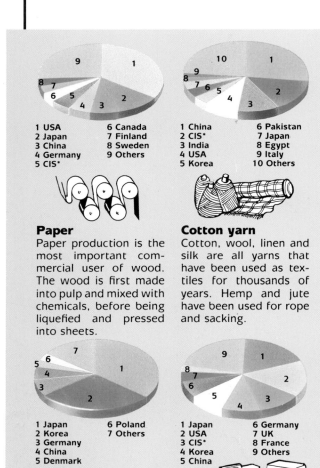

1 USA	6 Canada
2 Japan	7 Finland
3 China	8 Sweden
4 Germany	9 Others
5 CIS*	

Paper
Paper production is the most important commercial user of wood. The wood is first made into pulp and mixed with chemicals, before being liquefied and pressed into sheets.

1 China	6 Pakistan
2 CIS*	7 Japan
3 India	8 Egypt
4 USA	9 Italy
5 Korea	10 Others

Cotton yarn
Cotton, wool, linen and silk are all yarns that have been used as textiles for thousands of years. Hemp and jute have been used for rope and sacking.

1 CIS*	6 Italy
2 Japan	7 Brazil
3 USA	8 France
4 China	9 Others
5 Germany	

Steel
Steel is made from iron mixed with carbon. Nickel, chromium, tungsten, cobalt or other metals are added if the steel is to be stainless, or very strong.

1 Japan	6 Poland
2 Korea	7 Others
3 Germany	
4 China	
5 Denmark	

Shipbuilding
A decline in world shipping has closed shipyards around the world. However, the oil industry has provided work, with orders for drilling rigs and supertankers (giant carriers of crude oil).

1 Japan	6 Germany
2 USA	7 UK
3 CIS*	8 France
4 Korea	9 Others
5 China	

Electronic goods
Radios, cassette players, stereos, video recorders, television sets, compact disc systems, home computers and calculators are the basis of today's vast electronic goods industry.

1 Japan	6 Spain
2 USA	7 CIS*
3 Germany	8 UK
4 France	9 Others
5 Italy	

Cars
Invented in Europe, the car was first mass-produced in the United States, by Henry Ford (1863–1947). The car has revolutionized transportation and daily life in most parts of the world.

Chief producers of important minerals

Ag	Silver
Al	Bauxite
Au	Gold
Cr	Chromium
Cu	Copper
Fe	Iron
Ni	Nickel
Pb	Lead
Sn	Tin
Zn	Zinc
◆	Diamonds

1 CIS*	6 Iran
2 USA	7 Iraq
3 Saudi Arabia	8 Canada
4 Mexico	9 Venezuela
5 China	10 Others

1 CIS*	6 USA
2 Brazil	7 Canada
3 Australia	8 Others
4 China	
5 India	

1 Chile	6 Zambia
2 USA	7 Poland
3 Canada	8 Peru
4 CIS*	9 Australia
5 Zaïre	10 Others

1 Australia	7 Others
2 Guinea	
3 Jamaica	
4 CIS*	
5 Surinam	
6 Brazil	

1 Malaysia	6 China
2 Brazil	7 Bolivia
3 CIS*	8 Australia
4 Indonesia	9 Others
5 Thailand	

Oil
Oil, or petroleum, is found under the ground or beneath the sea bed and is raised by drilling. It is then refined for use as fuel, or processed and made into plastics, waxes, paints and synthetic fibres. Oil and gas provide about three-quarters of the world's energy.

Iron ore
This metal ore is mined in the Commonwealth of Independent States, Australia, the United States, and many other parts of the world. The ore is crushed, sorted and transported to a furnace, where it is burned at high temperatures to make steel.

Copper
Copper is used in telecommunications, heating and electrical systems, and many other areas of industry. It can be alloyed, or combined, with tin to produce bronze, and with tin, zinc and copper to produce brass.

Bauxite
Bauxite is the name of the ore that contains aluminium, a lightweight metal used widely in industry and shaped into cans, strips and wires. It is mined in the Caribbean, in Europe, Australia and the Commonwealth of Independent States.

Tin
Tin is widely used by the world's industrial nations. It is added to other metals to make alloys such as bronze, and used for coating steel to prevent rusting. Tin is mined in South America, southeast Asia, China, the Commonwealth of Independent States and Australia.

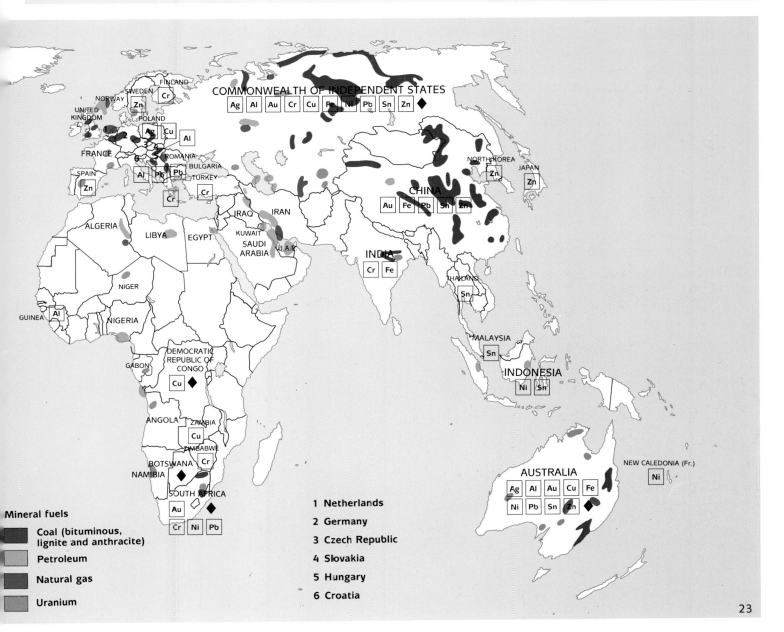

Mineral fuels

- Coal (bituminous, lignite and anthracite)
- Petroleum
- Natural gas
- Uranium

1 Netherlands
2 Germany
3 Czech Republic
4 Slovakia
5 Hungary
6 Croatia

EUROPE

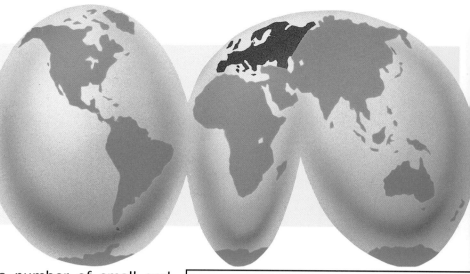

This continent is made up of a number of small and densely populated countries. It extends from the Scandinavian countries in the north, which lie partly within the Arctic Circle, to the Mediterranean countries in the south. Also included is the European part of Russia, west of the Ural mountains. Europe contains the world's smallest country, Vatican City, which has about 1000 inhabitants.

Climate and landscape differ enormously, from the cold uplands of Scandinavia and northern Russia, to the semi-desert conditions of parts of central Spain and southern Italy. A range of high mountains crosses southern Europe, forming the Pyrenees between France and Spain, the Alps (which run across Switzerland, France, Austria, Germany and Italy, and down the Adriatic coast to Albania), the Dolomites in Italy, and farther east the Tatra and Carpathian

cont. page 26

BELGIUM
Official name Royaume de Belgique, Koninkrijk België
Area 30,519 sq. km. (11,783 sq. miles)
Population 10,226,000
Capital Brussels (pop. 954,000)
Largest cities Antwerp (448,000)
Ghent (224,000)
Charleroi (202,000)
Liège (188,000)
Bruges (116,000)
Currency Euro
Official language(s) Dutch (Flemish) and French (Walloon)
Chief products Cement, chemicals, glass, soap, cutlery, paper, steel, textiles, meat products (especially ham and pâte), cereals, dairy products, fish
Exports Iron and steel, textiles, copper, plastic products
Imports Machinery, vehicles, diamonds, oil, food

DENMARK
Official name Kongeriget Danmark
Area 43,092 sq. km. (16,638 sq. miles)
Population 5,326,000
Capital Copenhagen (pop. 649,000)
Largest cities Århus (216,000)
Odense (145,000)
Ålborg (119,000)
Esbjerg (73,000)
Randers (56,000)
Kolding (53,000)
Currency Danish Krone
Official language(s) Danish
Chief products Dairy products, bacon, poultry, eggs, cereals, livestock, fish (especially cod, haddock, salmon), cement, diesel engines, electrical equipment, furniture, silverware
Exports Machinery, pork, other meat products, fish
Imports Machinery, manufactured goods, iron and steel, textiles

FRANCE
Official name République Française
Area 543,965 sq. km. (210,033 sq. miles)
Population 58,620,000
Capital Paris (pop. 2,152,000)
Largest cities Marseille (800,000)
Lyon (416,000)
Toulouse (359,000)
Nice (342,000)
Strasbourg (252,000)
Currency Euro
Official language(s) French (Breton and Basque are also spoken)
Chief products Aircraft, vehicles, aluminium, chemicals, electrical equipment, iron and steel, coal, jewellery, perfume, wine, cheese, cereals
Exports Machinery, vehicles, iron and steel, textiles, wheat, oil products, wine, cheese
Imports Machinery, oil, iron and steel, meat, textiles, fruit

THE NETHERLANDS
Official name Koninkrijk der Nederlanden
Area 41,160 sq. km. (15,891 sq. miles)
Population 16,805,000
Capital Amsterdam (pop. 715,000) (seat of government – The Hague)
Largest cities Rotterdam (590,000)
The Hague (443,000)
Utrecht (233,000)
Eindhoven (198,000)
Tilburg (186,000)
Currency Euro
Official language(s) Dutch
Chief products Natural gas, oil, salt, electrical equipment, clothing, iron and steel, machinery, vehicles, ships, dairy products, flowers, cereals
Exports Machinery, textiles, chemical products, meat, flowers, vegetables
Imports Crude oil, vehicles, iron and steel, clothing

UNITED KINGDOM
Official name The United Kingdom of Great Britain and Northern Ireland
Area 244,103 sq. km. (94,249 sq. miles)
Population 59,501,000
Capital London (pop. 7,285,000)
Largest cities Birmingham (1,014,000)
Leeds (727,000)
Glasgow (620,000)
Sheffield (530,000)
Currency Pound Sterling
Official language(s) English and Welsh
Chief products Oil, natural gas, coal, iron ore, steel, chalk, fish (especially cod, herring), chemicals, clothing, vehicles, cereals, machinery, dairy products
Exports Machinery, vehicles, textiles, electrical equipment, iron and steel, alcoholic drinks, aircraft
Imports Machinery, fruit and vegetables, diamonds, minerals, cereals, butter, meat, textiles

REPUBLIC OF IRELAND
Official name Eire
Area 68,895 sq. km.
(26,595 sq. miles)
Population 3,752,000
Capital Dublin
Official language(s) Irish
and English
Chief products Processed
foods, dairy products,
spirits, beer, paper and
paper products

ICELAND
Official name Island
Area 103,000 sq. km.
(39,769 sq. miles)
Population 278,000
Capital Reykjavik
Official language(s)
Icelandic, Danish
Chief products Fish and
fish products, cement,
aluminium, potatoes,
turnips

NORWAY
Official name Kongeriket
Norge
Area 323,878 sq. km.
(125,050 sq. miles)
Population 4,460,000
Capital Oslo
Official language(s)
Norwegian
Chief products Fish
(especially cod and herring),
timber, livestock, crude oil,
natural gas

SWEDEN
Official name
Konungariket Sverige
Area 440,945 sq. km.
(170,250 sq. miles)
Population 8,857,000
Capital Stockholm
Official language(s)
Swedish
Chief products Aircraft,
vehicles, timber, minerals

FINLAND
Official name Suomen
Tasavalta
Area 338,145 sq. km.
(130,559 sq. miles)
Population 5,166,000
Capital Helsinki
Official language(s)
Finnish and Swedish
Chief products Timber,
paper, textiles, metals

The vinyards of Château du Pavillon near Bordeaux, France.

EUROPE
Highest point Mount
Elbrus (Russia) 5633m.
(18,481ft.) above sea level
Lowest point Shore of
Caspian Sea 29m. (92ft.)
below sea level
Longest river Volga
(Russia) 3688km. (2290
miles)
Largest lake Lake Lagoda
(Russia) 18,389 sq. km.
(7100 sq. miles)

SPAIN
Official name España
Area 505,782 sq. km.
(194,897 sq. miles)
Population 39,140,000
Capital Madrid (pop.
2,881,000)
Largest cities Barcelona
(1,505,000)
Valencia (739,000)
Seville (701,000)
Zaragoza (603,000)
Málaga (528,000)
Currency Euro
Official language(s)
Spanish (Catalan, Basque
and Galician are also
spoken)
Chief products Vehicles,
cement, iron ore, clothing,
ships, steel, olives, wine,
grapes, oranges
Exports Machinery, citrus,
fruits, vegetables,
footwear, oil products,
textiles, ships, olive oil,
wine
Imports Crude oil,
machinery, iron and steel,
organic chemicals, corn,
soya, timber, copper

ITALY
Official name Repubblica
Italiana
Area 301,225 sq. km.
(116,300 sq. miles)
Population 57,746,000
Capital Rome (pop.
2,645,000)
Largest cities Milan
(1,308,000)
Naples (1,020,000)
Turin (910,000)
Palermo (686,000)
Currency Euro
Official language(s) Italian
Chief products Industrial
and office equipment,
domestic appliances,
vehicles, textiles, clothing,
chemicals, citrus fruits,
wheat, corn, olives, wine
Exports Machinery,
textiles, clothing, metals
(especially mercury),
chemicals, vehicles,
footwear, leather goods
Imports Chemicals, metals
and minerals, vehicles,
agricultural products, food,
machinery, oil

PORTUGAL
Official name República
Portuguesa
Area 91,630 sq. km.
(33,370 sq. miles)
Population 9,989,000
Capital Lisbon
Official language(s)
Portuguese
Chief products Ships,
textiles, citrus fruits, cork,
leather goods, port, fish
(especially sardines)

25

ranges. The highest mountain in the Alps is Mont Blanc which reaches 4813 metres, and which is situated on the border between France and Italy. Many famous rivers flow from these mountains. The Rhine has its source in the Swiss Alps and flows through Germany and the Netherlands. The Danube, which has its source in the Black Forest, flows east for 2858 kilometres through seven countries before reaching the Black Sea.

Much of lowland Europe is intensively cultivated, being given over mostly to cereal crops or dairy herds. Local variations, however, give different regions very distinctive characters: olive groves and vineyards are widespread in countries bordering the Mediterranean or the Black Sea. Fruit orchards and the production of pigs and poultry are common throughout Europe, particularly in areas close to large cities, the major markets for local produce.

Haystacks in the Balkan Mountains in Bulgaria.

Name	Area sq. km (sq. miles)	Population	Capital
Andorra	465 (180)	66,000	Andorra la Vella
Gibraltar (UK)	6.5 (2.125)	28,000	–
Liechtenstein	160 (62)	32,000	Vaduz
Malta	316 (122)	379,000	Valletta
Monaco	1.6 (0.65)	32,000	Monaco
San Marino	60.5 (23.4)	26,000	San Marino
Vatican City	0.44 (0.17)	1000	–

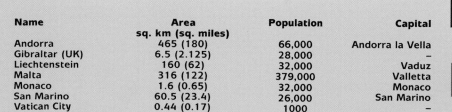
ANDORRA   MALTA   MONACO   VATICAN CITY

Note: Cyprus is defined here as part of Europe but appears also on the maps of Asia on pages 75 and 77. For Turkey's flag and details, see page 74.

GEORGIA
Area 69,700 sq. km.
(26,911 sq. miles)
Population 5,452,000
Capital Tbilisi

LATVIA
Area 63,959 sq. km.
(24,695 sq. miles)
Population 2,431,000
Capital Riga

CYPRUS
Area 9251 sq. km.
(3572 sq. miles)
Population 760,000
Capital Nicosia
Official language(s)
Greek and Turkish
Chief products Clothing, footwear, plastics, avocados

RUSSIA
Area 17,076,811 sq. km.
(6,593,391 sq. miles)
Population 146,195,000
Capital Moscow (pop. 9,270,000)
Largest cities
St. Petersburg (5,130,000)
Nizhny Novgorod (1,400,000)
Currency Ruble
Official language(s)
Russian, plus 38 minority languages
Chief products Coal, iron ore, minerals, oil, gas, steel, cereals, cotton

AUSTRIA
Area 83,855 sq. km.
(32,377 sq. miles)
Population 8,092,000
Capital Vienna
Official language(s)
German
Chief products Timber, chemicals, iron ore, steel

GERMANY
Official name Deutschland
Area 357,042 sq. km.
(137,855 sq. miles)
Population 82,100,000
Capital Berlin (pop. 3,447,000)
Largest cities Hamburg (1,707,000)
Munich (1,216,000)
Currency Euro
Official language(s)
German
Chief products Minerals, vehicles, steel, chemicals, clothing, electrical goods, livestock, beer, wine

POLAND
Area 312,683 sq. km.
(120,727 sq. miles)
Population 38,654,000
Capital Warsaw
Official language(s) Polish
Chief products Chemicals, iron, steel, ships, coal

ESTONIA
Area 45,099 sq. km.
(17,413 sq. miles)
Population 1,442,000
Capital Tallinn

ARMENIA
Area 29,800 sq. km.
(11,506 sq. miles)
Population 3,809,000
Capital Yerevan

ROMANIA
Area 237,500 sq. km.
(91,699 sq. miles)
Population 22,458,000
Capital Bucharest
Official language(s)
Romanian
Chief products Iron ore, oil, natural gas, machinery

GREECE
Area 131,957 sq. km.
(50,949 sq. miles)
Population 10,538,000
Capital Athens
Official language(s)
Greek
Chief products Bauxite, lignite, cotton, tobacco, citrus fruits, olives, textiles

AZERBAIJAN
Area 88,800 sq. km.
(33,436 sq. miles)
Population 7,983,000
Capital Baku

MOLDOVA
Area 33,700 sq. km.
(13,012 sq. miles)
Population 4,281,000
Capital Chişinău

The EU building in Brussels.

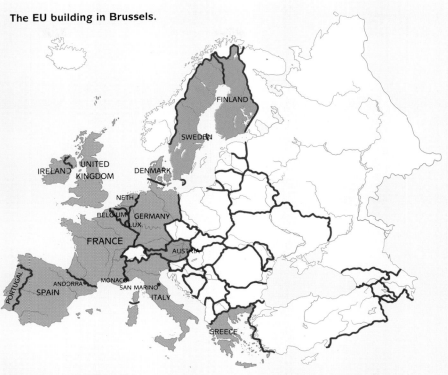

European Union

Fifteen countries in Europe are members of a group called the European Union. Its purpose is to promote economic co-operation and co-ordination between its member states, in order to help them compete on equal terms with the economies of the USA and Japan. In 1951 the European Coal and Steel Community (ECSC) was established. This led, in 1957, to the creation of the European Economic Community (EEC) itself. The European Parliament, formed in 1952, now has 626 members (MEPs), who are selected in local elections held in each country. The Parliament votes on economic policies relating to trade, agriculture and environmental issues.

By 1992 restrictions were lifted on the movement of capital, goods, services and workers, as well as tourists between member states. And in 1993, the Maastrict Treaty gave European citizenship to the people of all member countries.

Member countries of the European Union:
Austria
Belgium
Denmark
Finland
France
Germany
Greece
Republic of Ireland
Italy
Luxembourg
The Netherlands
Portugal
Spain
Sweden
United Kingdom

SWITZERLAND
Area 41,293 sq. km. (15,943 sq. miles)
Population 7,136,000
Capital Bern
Official language(s) German, French, Italian
Chief products Electrical equipment, chemicals

MACEDONIA
Area 25,713 sq. km. (9928 sq. miles)
Population 2,021,000
Capital Skopje

BELARUS
Area 207,976 sq. km. (80,300 sq. miles)
Population 10,032,000
Capital Minsk

LUXEMBOURG
Area 2585 sq. km. (998 sq. miles)
Population 432,000
Capital Luxembourg
Official language(s) French, Letzeburgish
Chief products Chemicals iron, machinery, paints

CZECH REPUBLIC
Area 78,864 sq. km. (30,450 sq. miles)
Population 10,278,000
Capital Prague

LITHUANIA
Area 67,787 sq. km. (26,173 sq. miles)
Population 3,699,000
Capital Vilnius
Chief products Wheat, timber, potatoes, electrical equipment

YUGOSLAVIA
Official name Federal Republic of Yugoslavia
Area 102,173 sq. km. (39,449 sq. miles)
Population 10,616,000
Capital Belgrade

CROATIA
Area 56,538 sq. km. (21,829 sq. miles)
Population 4,464,000
Capital Zagreb

BULGARIA
Area 110,912 sq. km. (42,823 sq. miles)
Population 8,208,000
Capital Sofia
Official language(s) Bulgarian
Chief products Cereals, electrical equipment, fruit

SLOVENIA
Area 20,251 sq. km. (7819 sq. miles)
Population 1,986,000
Capital Ljubljana

ALBANIA
Area 28,748 sq. km. (11,100 sq. miles)
Population 3,375,000
Capital Tiranë
Official language(s) Albanian
Chief products Textiles, oil products, wheat

BOSNIA AND HERCEGOVINA
Area 51,129 sq. km. (19,741 sq. miles)
Population 3,881,000
Capital Sarajevo

HUNGARY
Area 93,033 sq. km. (35,920 sq. miles)
Population 10,068,000
Capital Budapest
Official language(s) Hungarian
Chief products Coal, bauxite, wheat, sugar beet

SLOVAKIA
Area 49,035 sq. km. (18,932 sq. miles)
Population 5,396,000
Capital Bratislava

UKRAINE
Area 652,796 sq. km. (252,046 sq. miles)
Population 49,950,000
Capital Kiev
Chief products Grain, coal, iron and steel, sugar beet, machinery, chemicals

SCANDINAVIA AND FINLAND

The countries of Scandinavia (Norway, Sweden and Denmark), together with Finland and the island of Iceland, lie in the north of Europe. These countries have small populations and a high standard of living.

Norway, Sweden and Finland are all heavily forested, so lumbering – the felling of trees to make paper, furniture and other wood-based products – is an important industry. The warming influence of the Atlantic Gulf Stream brings with it huge shoals of cod, haddock, mackerel and herring; Norway, Denmark and Iceland all have large fishing industries. Norway has also benefited from the discovery, in 1970, of oil in the North Sea. Valuable supplies of iron ore and other minerals in Sweden supply its heavy industry, which produces ships, Volvo and Saab cars, and aeroplanes.

Iceland's volcanoes and geysers attract many tourists during the short summer, and much of this volcanic power is harnessed to produce electricity.

Danish farming
Cheese-making in Denmark. Danish agriculture is centred on cattle, pigs and chickens, and most of the crops grown in Denmark are used to feed the livestock.

Swedish logging mill
Trees are cut in the forests of Sweden and floated downstream to a logging mill where they are processed into pulp. This is then used to make paper.

A Norwegian fishing port
Sea fishing is one of Norway's most important industries. All the way up its long indented coastline there are fishing ports like this one, Hammerfest, in the far north of Norway.

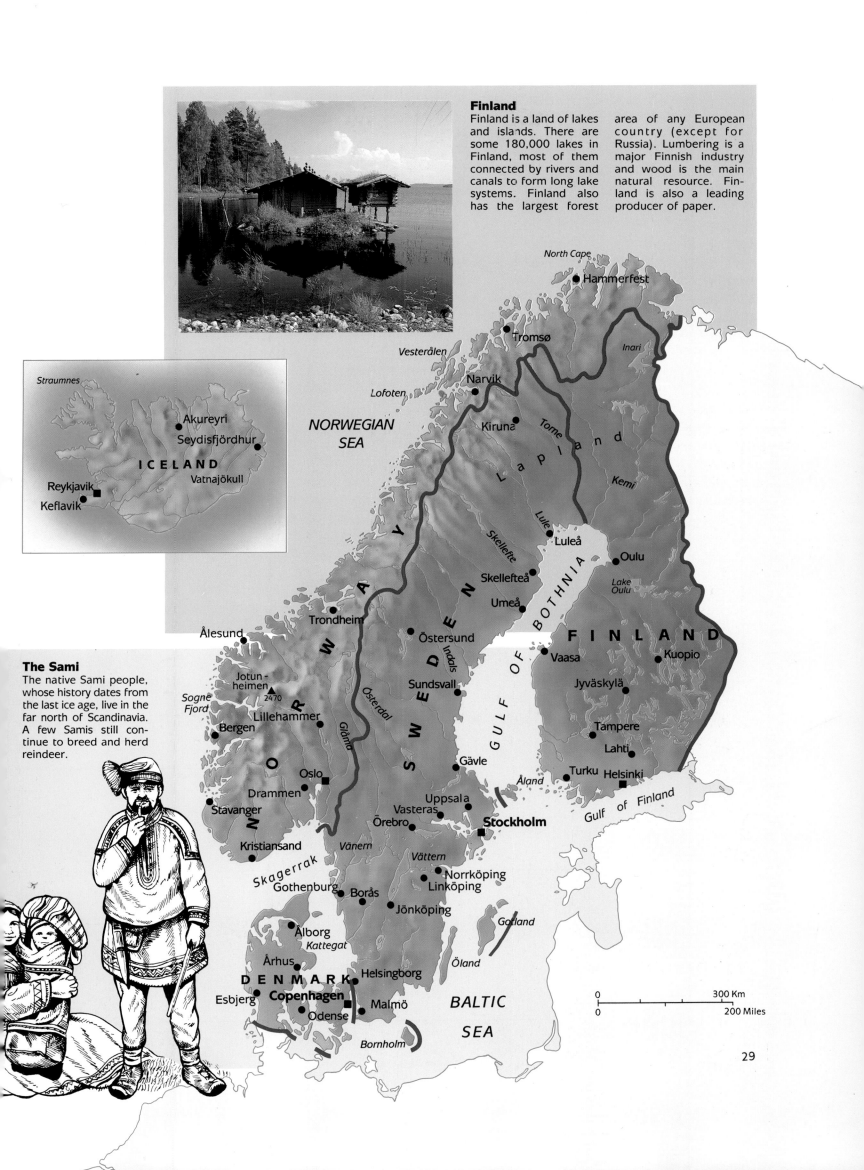

Finland

Finland is a land of lakes and islands. There are some 180,000 lakes in Finland, most of them connected by rivers and canals to form long lake systems. Finland also has the largest forest area of any European country (except for Russia). Lumbering is a major Finnish industry and wood is the main natural resource. Finland is also a leading producer of paper.

The Sami

The native Sami people, whose history dates from the last ice age, live in the far north of Scandinavia. A few Samis still continue to breed and herd reindeer.

Iceland map labels

Straumnes
Akureyri
Seydisfjördhur
ICELAND
Vatnajökull
Reykjavik
Keflavik

Main map labels

North Cape
Hammerfest
Tromsø
Vesterålen
Inari
Narvik
Lofoten
NORWEGIAN SEA
Kiruna
Tome
Lapland
Kemi
Lule
Skellefte
Luleå
Oulu
Skellefteå
Lake Oulu
Umeå
Trondheim
Östersund
GULF OF BOTHNIA
FINLAND
Ålesund
Vaasa
Kuopio
Indals
Sundsvall
Jyväskylä
Jotun-heimen
2470
Österdal
Sogne Fjord
Lillehammer
Tampere
Bergen
Lahti
Gävle
Turku
Helsinki
Glåma
Oslo
Åland
Drammen
Gulf of Finland
Uppsala
Stavanger
Vasteras
Örebro
Stockholm
Kristiansand
Vänern
Vättern
Skagerrak
Norrköping
Gothenburg
Linköping
Borås
Jönköping
Gotland
Ålborg
Kattegat
Öland
Århus
DENMARK
Helsingborg
Esbjerg
Copenhagen
BALTIC
Odense
Malmö
SEA
Bornholm

0   300 Km
0   200 Miles

29

BRITISH ISLES

The British Isles consist of the two main islands of Great Britain and Ireland, and a number of much smaller islands. The United Kingdom is made up of England, Wales, Scotland and Northern Ireland.

The position of the British Isles, near the warming influence of the Atlantic Gulf Stream, gives a mild climate. Cereal and vegetable crops grow well in the lowlands of southern England, while upland pastures in western and northern regions provide grazing for sheep and dairy cattle.

Britain's heavy industry grew up around the coalfields of central Scotland, northern England and south Wales. Ship-building, textile and steel-making industries were centred on cities such as Glasgow, Newcastle and Manchester, and Belfast in Northern Ireland. Now, half of Britain's exports come from the manufacture of electrical and engineering equipment, such as aircraft engines, cars, tractors and electronic devices. London, the capital of England, is a financial centre of international importance.

County Kerry, Ireland

The low green fields of central Ireland gradually rise to some of the highest peaks of the country on the south-western coast. The most westerly point in the British Isles is in County Kerry, where the full force of the Atlantic Ocean has made a rugged, indented coastline with high-sided river estuaries and many offshore islands. Ireland's countryside has remained unspoilt because it is not heavily industrialized.

The Lloyds Building, London

The Lloyds Building, built in 1986, houses the world's most famous insurance company. The company originated in 1688 in Edward Lloyd's coffee house.

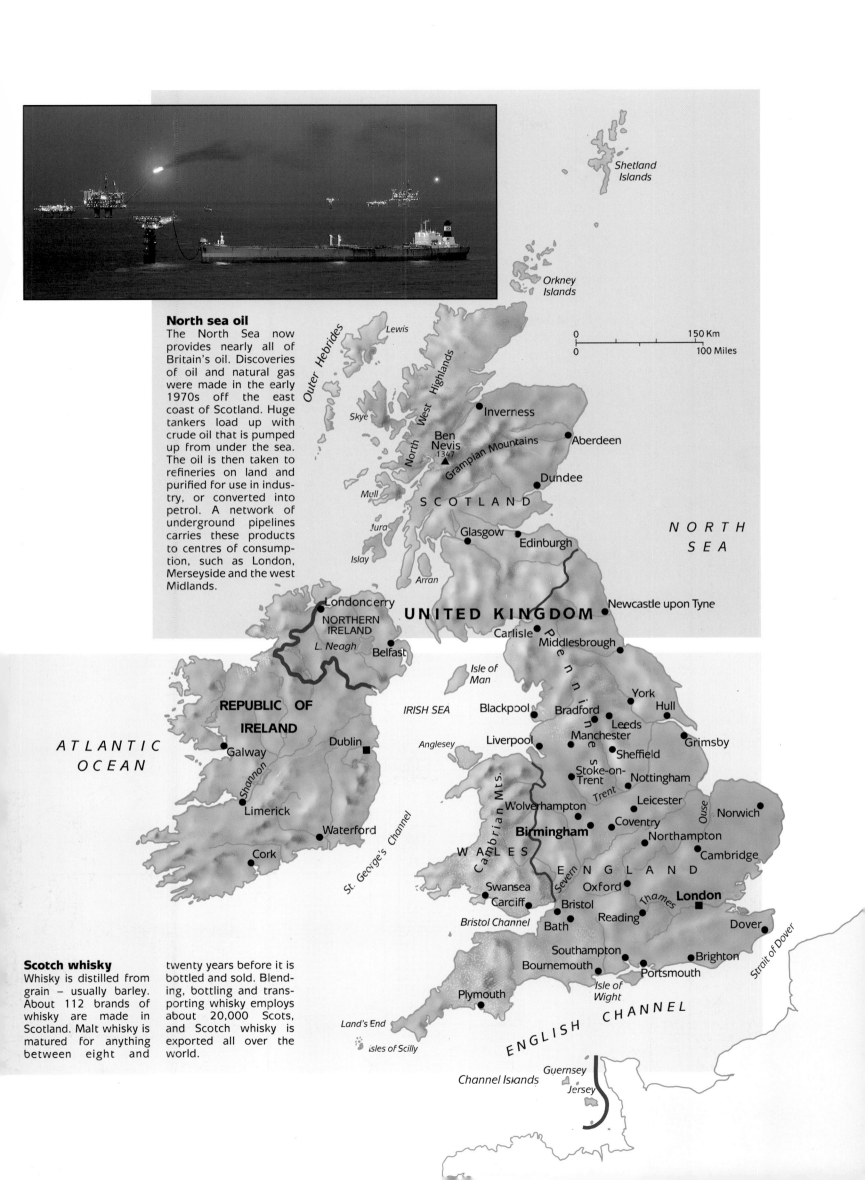

North sea oil

The North Sea now provides nearly all of Britain's oil. Discoveries of oil and natural gas were made in the early 1970s off the east coast of Scotland. Huge tankers load up with crude oil that is pumped up from under the sea. The oil is then taken to refineries on land and purified for use in industry, or converted into petrol. A network of underground pipelines carries these products to centres of consumption, such as London, Merseyside and the west Midlands.

Scotch whisky

Whisky is distilled from grain – usually barley. About 112 brands of whisky are made in Scotland. Malt whisky is matured for anything between eight and twenty years before it is bottled and sold. Blending, bottling and transporting whisky employs about 20,000 Scots, and Scotch whisky is exported all over the world.

Shetland Islands

Orkney Islands

150 Km

100 Miles

Outer Hebrides

Lewis

Skye

North West Highlands

Inverness

Ben Nevis 1347

Grampian Mountains

Aberdeen

Mull

Jura

Dundee

SCOTLAND

Islay

Glasgow

Edinburgh

NORTH SEA

Arran

Londonderry

NORTHERN IRELAND

L. Neagh

Belfast

UNITED KINGDOM

Newcastle upon Tyne

Carlisle

Middlesbrough

Pennines

Isle of Man

York

Hull

REPUBLIC OF IRELAND

IRISH SEA

Blackpool

Bradford

Leeds

Grimsby

ATLANTIC OCEAN

Galway

Dublin

Anglesey

Liverpool

Manchester

Sheffield

Stoke-on-Trent

Nottingham

Trent

Leicester

Norwich

Shannon

Limerick

Cambrian Mts.

Wolverhampton

Coventry

Ouse

Northampton

Waterford

WALES

Birmingham

ENGLAND

Cambridge

Cork

Severn

Swansea

Cardiff

Bristol

Oxford

Thames

London

St. George's Channel

Bristol Channel

Bath

Reading

Dover

Southampton

Brighton

Bournemouth

Portsmouth

Strait of Dover

Plymouth

Isle of Wight

Land's End

ENGLISH CHANNEL

Isles of Scilly

Channel Islands

Guernsey

Jersey

FRANCE

France is one of the richest nations in Europe, and is famous for its fine wines and good cooking. It is the largest country in western Europe and ninety per cent of its land is suitable for farming. The mild temperatures and rain from the Atlantic Ocean, and farther south the warmer Mediterranean climate, provide suitable conditions for the cultivation of wheat, maize, artichokes, vines and tobacco.

The main industrial region lies in the north-east where there are important steel and engineering industries, including the manufacture of Renault and Citroën cars. But there are also newer centres for high-tech industry in the south, in areas around Toulouse, Marseille and Grenoble. Paris, the capital of France, has been a world centre of art and learning for hundreds of years. Today, it is also well-known for designer fashion, and for its perfume industry.

France is a country of widely differing landscapes. The French Alps are popular for skiing, while the Riviera along the Mediterranean coast is a fashionable beach resort.

The Louvre
The Louvre in Paris was once one of the palaces of the kings of France. Today it is an art gallery, full of famous paintings, including Leonardo da Vinci's *Mona Lisa*, sculpture and antiquities. This glass pyramid was added in 1989 to the Louvre buildings, forming a new entrance hall. It was commissioned by the French president at the time, François Mitterrand.

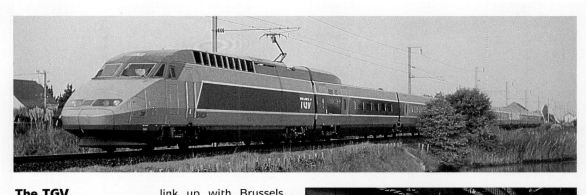

The TGV

The TGV was one of the first trains in the world to travel at 300 kilometres per hour. New railway lines have been specially laid for the train which runs from Paris to Lyon in two hours. It is part of a modern network of high-speed railways which will eventually link up with Brussels, Amsterdam, Cologne, and London via the Channel Tunnel. The picture on the right shows the TGV being constructed.

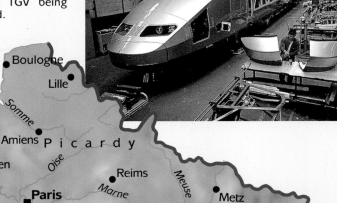

French wine

Vine cultivation is a cherished occupation in France. Each September the grapes are picked and taken to the presses. The grape juice slowly turns into high-quality wines such as Champagne, Burgundy and Bordeaux, which are named after the region they come from. French wines are exported all over the world.

The Tour de France

The Tour de France is the most popular sporting event in France. For three weeks in July, 150 cyclists race around France, climbing steep mountain roads and enduring high temperatures. A trail of TV camera crews, reporters, trainers and emergency services follows, and crowds line the route to offer their support.

Boulogne
Lille
Cherbourg
Le Havre
Somme
Amiens P i c a r d y
Rouen
Oise
Caen
Reims
Meuse
Marne
N o r m a n d y **Paris**
Metz
Nancy
Brest
Champagne
V o s g e s
Rennes
Seine
Troyes
Strasbourg
Quimper
B r i t t a n y
Le Mans
Orléans
Auxerre
Yonne
Mulhouse
St. Nazaire
Angers
Tours
Loire
Plateau de Langres
Doubs
Nantes
Cher
Bourges
Dijon
Besançon
Poitiers
Vienne
B u r g u n d y
Jura Mts.
F R A N C E
La Rochelle
B A Y
O F
B I S C A Y
Roanne
Saône
Mt. Blanc 4810
Limoges
Clermont-Ferrand
Angoulême
Puy de Sancy 1885
Allier
Lyon
Dordogne
St.-Étienne
Grenoble
Périgueux
M a s s i f
Bordeaux
C e n t r a l
Valence
A L P S
Lot
Garonne
Rhône
G a s c o n y
Nîmes
Avignon
Durance
Nice
Bayonne
Toulouse
Montpellier
Cannes
MONACO
Pau
Béziers
Marseille
Riviera
P y r e n e e s
Toulon
Perpignan
M E D I T E R R A N E A N
S E A
Bastia
Corsica
Ajaccio

0 ——— 200 Km
0 ——— 150 Miles

BENELUX

Benelux is a name given to a group of three countries. BElgium, the NEtherlands (often known as Holland) and LUXembourg. The landscape of Holland and parts of Belgium is very flat, crisscrossed by canals and waterways. About 7700 square kilometres of land in Holland have been reclaimed from the sea by draining away the water and building dykes and dams to keep the sea water out. Almost all the land is used for agriculture, specializing in dairy farming and horticulture.

All the Benelux countries are densely populated. Belgium is split between Dutch- and Flemish-speaking Flemings in the north and French-speaking Walloons in the south. A large proportion of these people work in industry. Despite the fact that most raw materials have to be imported, both Belgium and Luxembourg have heavy and light industries, producing metals, textiles and chemicals as well as more specialized products such as soap and cutlery.

Esch-sur-Sûre
The Sûre River cuts its path through the wooded hills around Esch-sur-Sûre in northern Luxembourg. This region of Luxembourg and the Ardennes region in south-east Belgium are well-known for their beautiful natural scenery. Groves of walnut trees hide slate-roofed villages and remote castles. The Ardennes region is also renowned for its ham and pâté.

Rotterdam

Rotterdam is the world's busiest port. It is situated at the mouth of the Rhine and Maas rivers which serve the industrial heartlands of Europe. Goods from the industrial Ruhr region of Germany, for example, are taken downstream by barge to Rotterdam where they are lifted by crane on to ocean-going vessels. Huge oil tankers arrive from the Middle East bringing crude oil for the oil refineries and the many related petro-chemical plants that are located here. The Dutch oil company, Shell, can now send oil by pipeline direct from its refinery at the harbour to Amsterdam, Antwerp and Germany. However, it is shipbuilding that is the most important industry in Rotterdam. Ever since the seventeenth century when the Dutch started trading with the Far East, skilled craft-workers have been building merchant vessels. Today, their expertise is sought throughout the world by countries that need large container ships and supertankers.

Alkmaar cheese market

Alkmaar, a town near Amsterdam, is famous for its cheese market. Every Friday from April to October cheeses are put on display by cheese-porters who still wear a traditional costume dating from the sixteenth century. Alkmaar is a centre for the dairy industry which is the main form of agriculture in the Netherlands. The warm waters of the Gulf Stream bring mild winters and wet summers which help to produce a long growing season and excellent grazing land for cattle.

The Atomium

The Atomium is an aluminium structure that was built for the World Fair in 1958 in Brussels. It is intended to represent a molecule of an iron crystal, magnified 265 million times. Each sphere is an atom, making up a total of nine atoms in the molecule. The three lower atoms now house an exhibition on the peaceful use of nuclear energy. You can take escalators up the tubes to reach a restaurant in the top sphere.

GERMANY

After World War II Germany was divided into two – the Federal Republic of Germany (West Germany), and the German Democratic Republic (East Germany), which traded almost exclusively with other Eastern European countries. In 1989, restrictions on freedom of travel and communication between the two countries were lifted for the first time since the war, and Germany was officially united on 3 October 1990.

Germany is a leading industrial nation. It has large natural reserves of coal and iron ore, and the Ruhr valley is one of the most important industrial centres in Europe. The Rhine is a vital route for industrial cargo, handled by ports such as Mannheim, Cologne and Duisburg. Germany also has traditional centres of manufacturing such as Dresden, famous for its china.

The northern region of Germany is a lowland plain – farther south the land is more mountainous and heavily forested. The coniferous forests and remote castles of the Black Forest and Bavarian Alps attract many tourists.

Coal-cutting in the Ruhr
Lignite, also known as brown coal, is being excavated at this open-cast mine in the Ruhr district. Modern equipment can dig out the coal quickly and efficiently. The Ruhr is one of the largest industrial areas in Europe.

Rothenburg on the Tauber
Rothenburg on the Tauber is in Bavaria in the south of Germany. It is one of the best preserved medieval towns in Germany, and little has changed in 400 years. All its walls, towers, high-gabled houses and narrow crooked streets date from that time. Traditional crafts such as woodcarving are still practised.

German industry

Germany is one of the biggest industrial nations in the world. It is well-known for its manufacturing of electrical equipment, machinery, chemicals and cars such as BMW and Volkswagen. However, despite the natural resources of areas such as the Ruhr valley, most fuel and other raw materials are in short supply and must be imported.

The Brandenburg Gate

The Brandenburg Gate stands to the east side of the now dismantled Berlin Wall. It has changed from being a symbol of German division to one of German unity. The Berlin Wall was put up after World War II to partition the city of Berlin.

East Berlin became the capital of East Germany, but West Berlin became an isolated pocket of West Germany inside the East German frontier. Until 1989 no-one, from the East or West, could cross the Wall except under special circumstances. Now the Wall has been pulled down and families and friends who were separated for over 40 years are free to see each other again.

0 _____ 200 Km
0 _____ 150 Miles

NORTH SEA

BALTIC SEA

Flensburg
Rügen
Kiel
Stralsund
Lübeck
Rostock
Wilhelmshaven
Schwerin
Hamburg
Oldenburg
Bremen
Elbe
Ems
Lower Saxony
Weser
Osnabrück
Hannover
Braunschweig
Berlin
Oder
Potsdam
Bielefeld
Magdeburg
Frankfurt
Münster
Salzgitter
Harz Mts.
Cottbus
Dortmund
Duisburg
Essen
Ruhr
Kassel
Halle
Elbe
Leipzig
Dresden
Düsseldorf
GERMANY
Cologne
Errurt
Zwickau
Chemnitz
Bonn
Rhine
Thuringian Forest
Eifel
Moselle
Wiesbaden
Frankfurt
Main
Mainz
Würzburg
Bohemian Forest
Mannheim
Neckar
Saarbrücken
Nürnberg
Karlsruhe
Regensburg
Stuttgart
Isar
Bavaria
Black Forest
Danube
Augsburg
Munich
Freiburg
L. Constance
ALPS

37

AUSTRIA AND SWITZERLAND

Austria and Switzerland are the most mountainous countries in Europe, with the Alps covering three-quarters of their land. Much of the people's way of life is dictated by this environment.

Since the sixteenth century Switzerland has had a policy of neutrality in times of war. This reputation for neutrality and security has made Switzerland one of the world's most important centres for banking.

Neither Austria nor Switzerland has reserves of oil or coal, and as a result water-power from the mountain rivers is a vital source of energy. Austria also relies heavily on Eastern European countries for its energy supplies. Swiss workers make high-quality products such as watches and scientific instruments, while Austria has big chemical and manufacturing industries. Tourism is extremely important in both countries: there are many famous ski resorts, and Vienna, the capital of Austria, is one of the great cultural centres of the world.

Swiss commerce
Switzerland has long had a tradition of neutrality and security. As a result it has become an important centre for international commerce and banking. The Swiss city, Geneva, is also the European headquarters for international organizations such as the Red Cross and the United Nations, and it has often been used by other countries to stage peace talks.

Ski-school at Verbier

Most Swiss children feel at home on skis by the age of seven. Local primary schools give lessons on the slopes, and there are special ski-schools to develop technique at an early age. Verbier is a big ski resort which attracts skiers from all over Europe every winter.

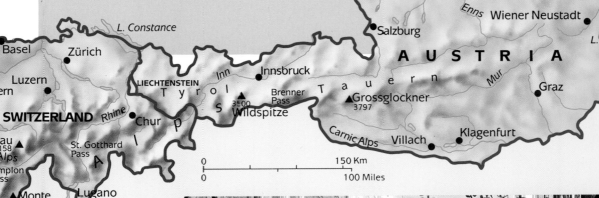

The Tyrol

The far western arm of Austria is part of a region known as the Tyrol. It is one of the highest Alpine areas and also one of the most traditional. The province was founded in the fourteenth century and is still regarded by its inhabitants as distinct from the modern states of Austria and Italy across which it lies.

Prater Park

This fairground wheel in Prater Park in Vienna, the capital of Austria, is one of the largest in Europe.

Salzburg

Salzburg lies just inside the border between Austria and Germany. It is the birthplace of the famous composer, Wolfgang Amadeus Mozart. Every summer there is a music festival in celebration of Mozart's operas and chamber music. Thousands of people come from all over Europe to enjoy the festival, and all the restaurants and hotels are full.

ITALY

Italy juts into the Mediterranean Sea and includes the two islands of Sicily at its foot, and Sardinia to the west. It is one of the youngest countries in Europe – its various kingdoms were not united until 1870.

Italy ranks among the richer nations of the world, yet there is a huge difference between the standard of living in the prosperous, industrial north and the poorer, mainly agricultural south. Rome may be the capital of Italy, but Milan in the north is its business, financial and industrial capital, and an international centre for fashion and design. In addition trades such as glass-blowing, shoe-making and weaving textiles for high-quality clothes are still practised in various traditional centres. However, Italy has limited natural resources and imports both oil and electricity.

In the south, olives and citrus fruits are grown, but the most fertile agricultural area is the Po valley in the north. Vines are grown on the slopes of the Apennine mountains.

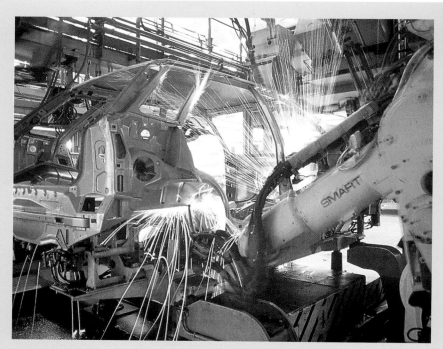

Vatican City
The Vatican is a separate city within Rome, from where the Pope leads the Roman Catholic Church worldwide. As well as being the smallest country in the world, with an area of less than one square kilometre, it is also the only place where Latin is the official language. It has its own bank, telephone and postal system as well as a small army called the Swiss Guard to protect the Pope himself.

Italy's industry
Italy's biggest manufacturing company is Fiat Motor Cars based in Turin. This company has one of the most up-to-date methods of car production in the world. Robots are used for complete precision in every process – assembling, welding and painting.

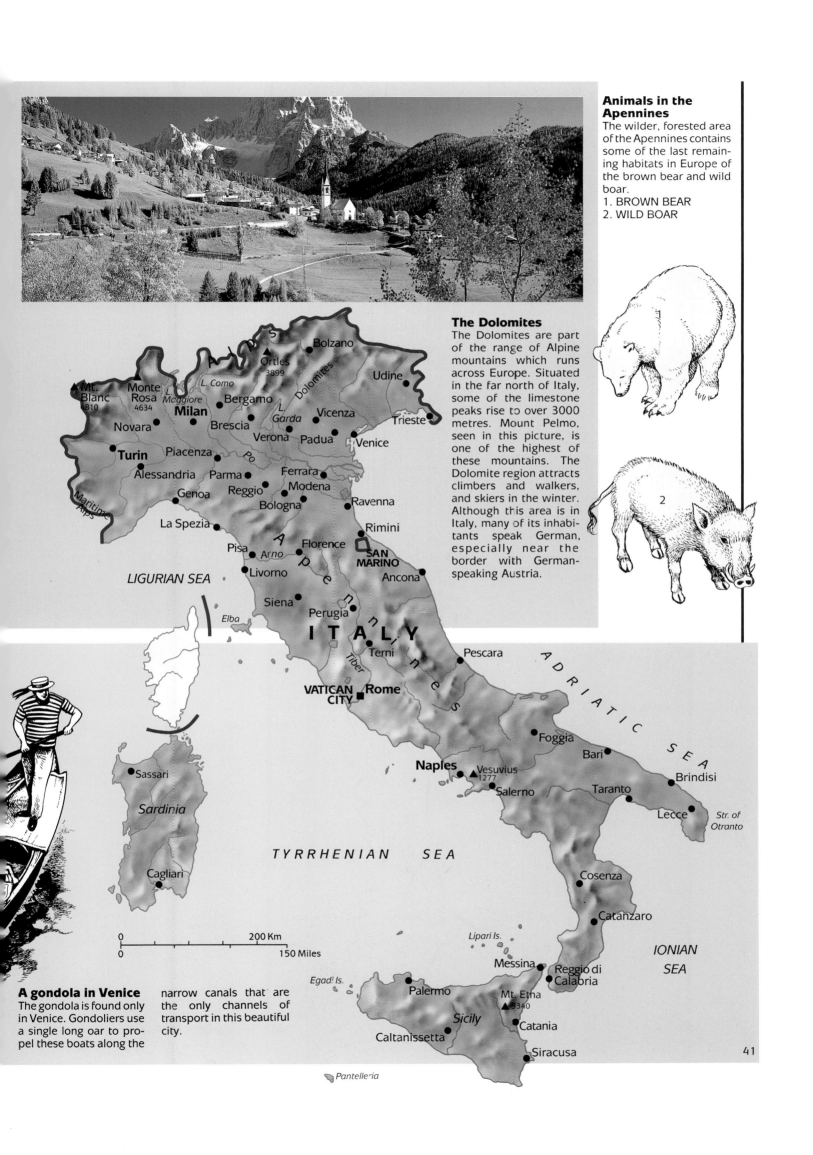

Animals in the Apennines
The wilder, forested area of the Apennines contains some of the last remaining habitats in Europe of the brown bear and wild boar.
1. BROWN BEAR
2. WILD BOAR

The Dolomites
The Dolomites are part of the range of Alpine mountains which runs across Europe. Situated in the far north of Italy, some of the limestone peaks rise to over 3000 metres. Mount Pelmo, seen in this picture, is one of the highest of these mountains. The Dolomite region attracts climbers and walkers, and skiers in the winter. Although this area is in Italy, many of its inhabitants speak German, especially near the border with German-speaking Austria.

A gondola in Venice
The gondola is found only in Venice. Gondoliers use a single long oar to propel these boats along the narrow canals that are the only channels of transport in this beautiful city.

Bolzano
Ortles 3899
Udine
Mt. Blanc 4810
Monte Rosa 4634
L. Maggiore
L. Como
Dolomites
Milan
Bergamo
Vicenza
Trieste
Novara
L. Garda
Verona
Padua
Venice
Turin
Piacenza
Brescia
Po
Alessandria
Parma
Ferrara
Maritime Alps
Genoa
Reggio
Modena
Bologna
Ravenna
La Spezia
Rimini
Pisa
Florence
Arno
SAN MARINO
LIGURIAN SEA
Livorno
Ancona
Siena
Elba
Perugia
ITALY
Apennines
Terni
Tiber
Pescara
VATICAN CITY
Rome
ADRIATIC SEA
Foggia
Bari
Naples
Vesuvius 1277
Brindisi
Sassari
Salerno
Taranto
Lecce
Str. of Otranto
Sardinia
TYRRHENIAN SEA
Cagliari
Cosenza
Catanzaro
IONIAN SEA
Lipari Is.
0 200 Km
0 150 Miles
Messina
Reggio di Calabria
Egadi Is.
Palermo
Mt. Etna 3340
Sicily
Catania
Caltanissetta
Siracusa

41

Pantelleria

SPAIN AND PORTUGAL

In the south-west corner of Europe, Spain and Portugal form the Iberian Peninsula. Spain is the second largest country in western Europe but it has only the fifth largest population. Spanish is one of four languages spoken – and almost a quarter of the Spanish speakers use dialects other than the official Castilian Spanish.

Since 1930 much of the Spanish population has moved away from the countryside to live and work in the cities and industrial centres. The chemical industry, shipbuilding, steel production and tourism are all important for Spain's economy. Spain also exports agricultural products, including olive oil, citrus fruit, and sherry from the Jerez region.

Portugal was less developed than Spain, but industry is now becoming more important. Tourism and the export of textiles are the traditional mainstays; in addition most of Europe's supply of cork comes from special oak trees in the south of the country.

Olive groves in Andalusia
Olives, which need little water, grow well in Andalusia in the south of Spain, where it is hot and dry. Most are crushed to make olive oil.

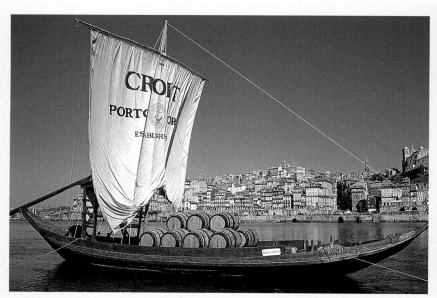

Oporto port
Portugal is famous for its port, a dark red wine usually drunk after dinner. It is made at vineyards along the river Douro, then put into casks and taken downstream by barge to Oporto, the city after which the wine is named. Here, the port is stored in cellars, called Lodges, and may be left to mature for ten to twenty years before being shipped all over the world.

Bullfighting
Every Sunday evening in Spain during the summer, crowds assemble in bullrings around the country. They watch and cheer as their favourite matador flicks his scarlet cape at the charging bull.

Spanish animals

The Spanish lynx is a long-legged wild cat that lives in the forest and preys on birds and small mammals. Red foxes are common in much of Europe.
1. SPANISH LYNX
2. RED FOX

Bilbao

Bilbao is a major Spanish port situated in northern Spain. Iron ore was discovered in Bilbao in the nineteenth century, and the town fast became an industrial centre with iron and steel foundries and shipbuilding yards. Bilbao is also the centre for the Basque movement ETA (Euskadi ta Askatasuna, meaning Freedom for the Basque Homeland), which agitates for independence from Spain.

SOUTH-EAST EUROPE

Romania, Bulgaria, Greece, Albania and the countries that emerged from the former Socialist Federal Republic of Yugoslavia – Croatia, Bosnia and Hercegovina, Slovenia, Macedonia, and the new Federal Republic of Yugoslavia – are known as the Balkan countries. They lie in south-east Europe, close to Asia. In the past many different ethnic groups have settled in this area, resulting in the present mix of people, languages and religions.

Much of the region is mountainous. The river Danube, which forms part of the boundary between Romania and Bulgaria, is surrounded by fertile, heavily-cultivated land. Much of the produce is sold in local markets but Bulgaria exports agricultural goods such as canned fruits and vegetables, and Greece exports olive oil and citrus fruits. Greece is a major shipping nation and tourist destination.

Throughout the 1990s and early 2000s, inter-ethnic tensions resulted in civil war among the peoples of former Yugoslavia. United Nations troops tried to restore peace. The conflict badly damaged the area's tourist industry.

A fruit market in Dubrovnik
Dubrovnik, an old, walled sea-port situated on the Adriatic coast, has long been known as a market for products such as cheese, milk, wood, olives and grapes brought from neighbouring villages.

Meteora, Greece
There are many monasteries in the beautiful mountainous countryside of Greece. The monasteries at Meteora in central Greece are set on top of a pinnacle of rock. To reach them, before steps were cut, people were hauled up the side in a basket.

44

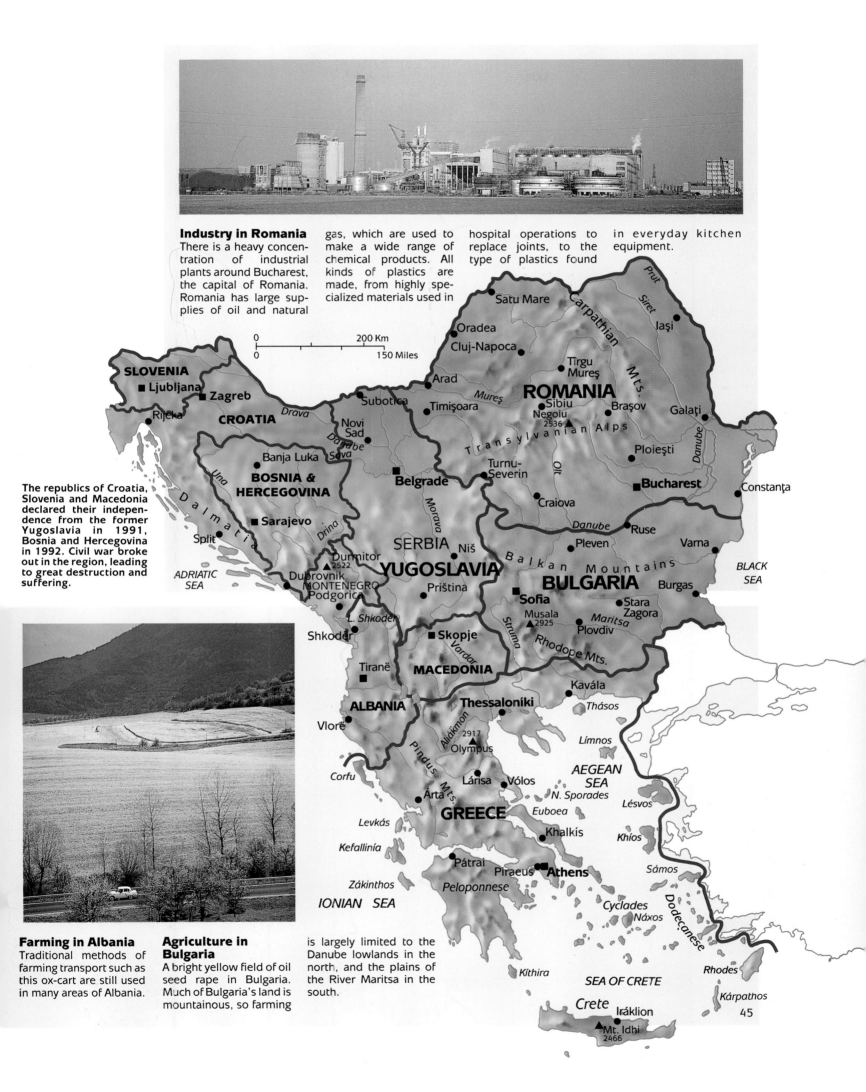

Industry in Romania
There is a heavy concentration of industrial plants around Bucharest, the capital of Romania. Romania has large supplies of oil and natural gas, which are used to make a wide range of chemical products. All kinds of plastics are made, from highly specialized materials used in hospital operations to replace joints, to the type of plastics found in everyday kitchen equipment.

The republics of Croatia, Slovenia and Macedonia declared their independence from the former Yugoslavia in 1991, Bosnia and Hercegovina in 1992. Civil war broke out in the region, leading to great destruction and suffering.

0   200 Km
0   150 Miles

SLOVENIA
Ljubljana
Zagreb
Rijeka
CROATIA
Drava
Subotica
Novi Sad
Danube
Sava
Banja Luka
BOSNIA & HERCEGOVINA
Una
Sarajevo
Split
Dalmatia
Dubrovnik
Durmitor 2522
MONTENEGRO
Podgorica
L. Shkodër
Shkodër
Drina
Morava
SERBIA
Niš
YUGOSLAVIA
Priština
Belgrade
Skopje
MACEDONIA
Vardar
Tiranë
ALBANIA
Vlorë
Corfu
Pindus Mts.
Árta
Levkás
Kefallinía
Zákinthos
IONIAN SEA
Olympus 2917
Aliákmon
Lárisa
Vólos
GREECE
Pátrai
Piraeus
Athens
Peloponnese
Kíthira
Crete
Iráklion
Mt. Idhi 2466

Satu Mare
Oradea
Cluj-Napoca
Arad
Mureş
Timişoara
ROMANIA
Tîrgu Mureş
Sibiu
Negoiu 2536
Braşov
Transylvanian Alps
Olt
Turnu-Severin
Craiova
Danube
Ploieşti
Bucharest
Constanţa
Ruse
Prut
Siret
Iaşi
Carpathian Mts.
Galaţi
Danube
Pleven
Varna
Balkan Mountains
Sofia
Musala 2925
Stara Zagora
Struma
Maritsa
Plovdiv
Rhodope Mts.
BULGARIA
Burgas
BLACK SEA
Kavála
Thessaloníki
Thásos
Limnos
AEGEAN SEA
N. Sporades
Lésvos
Euboea
Khalkís
Khíos
Sámos
Cyclades
Náxos
Dodecanese
SEA OF CRETE
Rhodes
Kárpathos

Farming in Albania
Traditional methods of farming transport such as this ox-cart are still used in many areas of Albania.

Agriculture in Bulgaria
A bright yellow field of oil seed rape in Bulgaria. Much of Bulgaria's land is mountainous, so farming is largely limited to the Danube lowlands in the north, and the plains of the River Maritsa in the south.

45

CENTRAL EUROPE

The Czech Republic and Slovakia – the former country of Czechoslovakia dissolved peacefully into two independent nations in 1993 – plus Poland and Hungary form part of central Europe. Poland and Hungary are mainly lowland countries; the Czech Republic and Slovakia are more mountainous. The climate in this region is temperate, but winters are cold, and ice often closes harbours along the Polish Baltic coast.

Poland, the Czech Republic and Slovakia are rich in natural resources and are all heavily industrialized. Poland mines coal, mainly from Silesia, which is both exported and used to supply the steel and shipbuilding industries based around Gdansk. Large deposits of gold were found near Prague in the mid-1980s; uranium is also mined in the mountains and used to produce nuclear power.

South of Budapest, the capital city of Hungary, the land surrounding the river Danube is particularly fertile and crops such as wheat, sugar beet and potatoes are grown.

Charles Bridge, Prague
The city of Prague, capital of the Czech Republic, was a major European cultural centre in medieval times. Much of the beautiful architecture remains, and now the old palaces house government institutions and academies of music and art.

Refining oil
This maze of pipes and tanks is necessary for the complex process of oil production. The Czech Republic, Slovakia, Poland and Hungary do not have large natural reserves of oil, so all four countries are forced to import crude oil from abroad. When crude oil is taken from below the ground or sea it has to be refined, so that it can be separated into oil, petrol, paraffin, and other products. This oil refinery is in Szazhalombatta, near Budapest, the capital of Hungary.

Polish traditional dress
In some rural areas Polish men and women still wear traditional dress. The strong, well-made garments last for a long time. These costumes are also worn for festivals and folk-dances which are an important part of popular culture all over Eastern Europe. Especially in the rural areas, traditional customs have been passed down from generation to generation and kept alive.

Agriculture in Poland

Rolling green fields typical of Poland's central agricultural region. Most of the farmland is planted with crops to grow feed for pigs and chickens. Farming machinery is usually old-fashioned and frequently there are no fertilizers to help crops to grow in the poorer soils. Distribution of farm produce to the market centres can also be difficult. There are sometimes food shortages and people often have to queue for hours to buy meat or bread.

BALTIC SEA

Gdynia

Gulf of Gdańsk

Gdańsk

Elblag

Pomerania

Olsztyn

Szczecin

Bydgoszcz

Toruń

Białystok

Vistula

Oder

P O L A N D

Poznań

Płock

Warsaw

Bug

Warta

Zielona Góra

Łódź

Radom

Lublin

Wrocław

Kielce

Walbrzych

Oder

Ore Mountains

Sudetes

Opole

Silesia

Bytom

Vistula

Katowice

Tarnów

Rzeszów

Prague

Plzeň

CZECH

B o h e m i a

Olomouc

Ostrava

Kraków

REPUBLIC

Bohemian Forest

Vltava

Brno

Carpathian Mts.

České Budějovice

Tatra Mts.

Váh

SLOVAKIA

Košice

Hron

Bratislava

Miskolc

Győr

Tisza

Budapest

Debrecen

HUNGARY

Kecskemét

L. Balaton

Drava

Danube

Szeged

Pécs

0   150 Km

0   100 Miles

47

FORMER SOVIET UNION

In December of 1991 the Union of Soviet Socialist Republics (USSR) ceased to exist as a single country. Formed after the Russian Revolution of 1917, it was made up of 15 republics. They are now independent countries, 12 of which still maintain contact through an organisation called the Commonwealth of Independent States.

Russia, the largest new country, is also the largest country in the world, stretching across the globe from Europe in the west to the Pacific Ocean in the east. The Ural Mountains, running north to south, divide the country into a European part and an Asian part. Thirty-eight national minorities make up about twenty per cent of the non-Russian population of the area that was the USSR.

cont. page 50

Russian Orthodox priests leading a service
After 70 years of repression by the government, religious life in Russia is now flourishing.

48

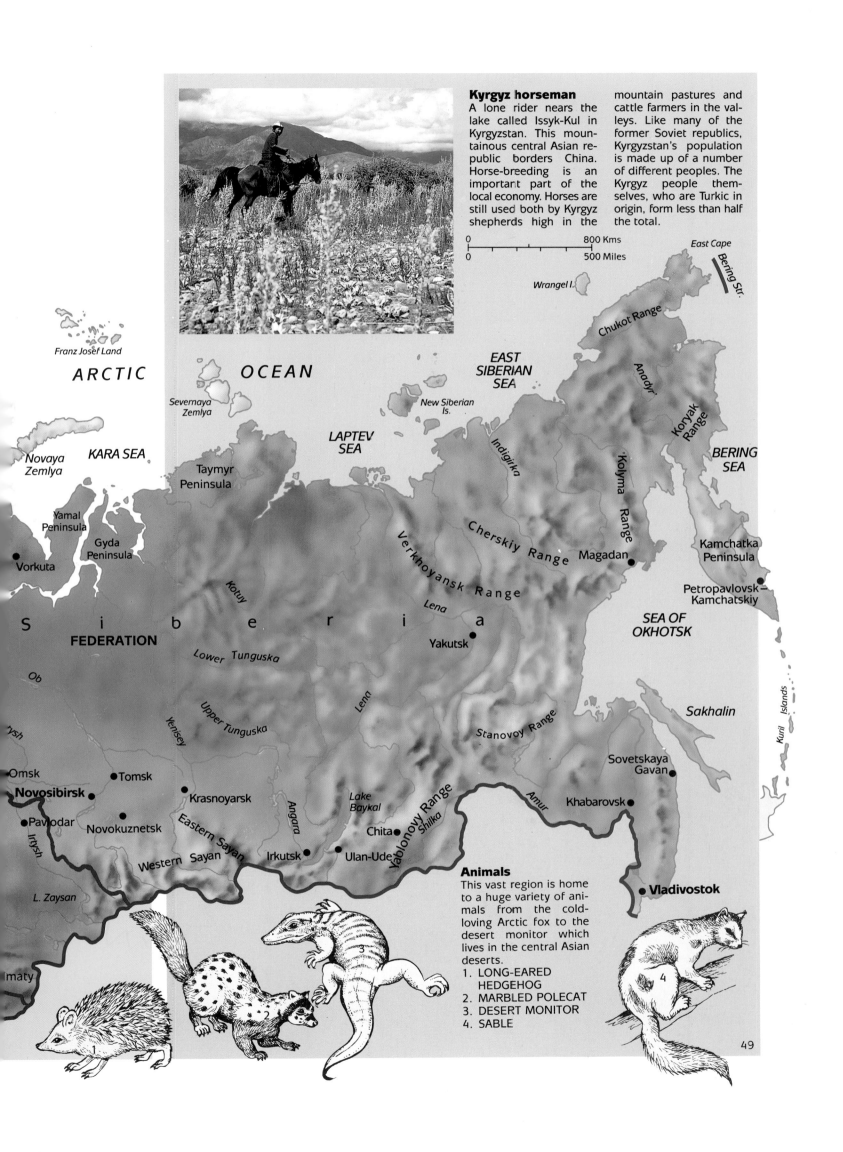

Kyrgyz horseman
A lone rider nears the lake called Issyk-Kul in Kyrgyzstan. This mountainous central Asian republic borders China. Horse-breeding is an important part of the local economy. Horses are still used both by Kyrgyz shepherds high in the mountain pastures and cattle farmers in the valleys. Like many of the former Soviet republics, Kyrgyzstan's population is made up of a number of different peoples. The Kyrgyz people themselves, who are Turkic in origin, form less than half the total.

0   800 Kms
0   500 Miles

East Cape

Wrangel I.

ARCTIC

Franz Josef Land

OCEAN

Severnaya Zemlya

EAST SIBERIAN SEA

Bering Str.

New Siberian Is.

LAPTEV SEA

Chukot Range

Anadyr

KARA SEA

Novaya Zemlya

Taymyr Peninsula

Indigirka

Koryak Range

BERING SEA

Yamal Peninsula

Cherskiy Range

Kolyma Range

Magadan

Kamchatka Peninsula

Gyda Peninsula

● Vorkuta

Verkhoyansk Range

Kotuy

Lena

Petropavlovsk–Kamchatskiy

SEA OF OKHOTSK

S   i   b   e   r   i   a

FEDERATION

Yakutsk

Ob

Lower   Tunguska

Lena

Sakhalin

Irtysh

Yenisey

Upper Tunguska

Stanovoy Range

Kuril Islands

● Omsk

● Tomsk

Sovetskaya Gavan

Novosibirsk ●

Angara

Krasnoyarsk ●

Lake Baykal

Yablonovy Range

Amur

Khabarovsk ●

● Pavlodar

Novokuznetsk ●

Eastern Sayan

Shilka

Chita ●

Irtysh

Western Sayan

Irkutsk ●

Ulan-Ude ●

L. Zaysan

Vladivostok

Almaty

Animals
This vast region is home to a huge variety of animals from the cold-loving Arctic fox to the desert monitor which lives in the central Asian deserts.
1. LONG-EARED HEDGEHOG
2. MARBLED POLECAT
3. DESERT MONITOR
4. SABLE

49

Winter in the northern city of St. Petersburg is long and cold.

The European countries are the most densely populated and contain well-developed heavy industries, such as coal-mining and steel manufacturing. The steel provides raw material for the manufacturing industries around Moscow and the shipbuilding industry in St. Petersburg. In the southern republics, agriculture is more dominant. Ukraine and Kazakhstan contain major grain-growing areas. However, massive amounts of food still have to be imported in order to feed their populations.

Russia's vast eastern region is sparsely populated, but has valuable resources of gas, coal and oil. However, the inhospitable terrain makes these resources difficult to tap. Another important energy resource is hydroelectric power from the river Volga. This river, the longest in Europe, provides transportation for both people and materials. The Trans-Siberian Railway, which connects Moscow with the Pacific coast many thousands of miles to the east, is also a vital communication link.

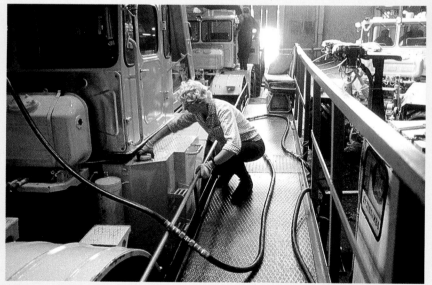

The Moscow Metro
The Moscow Metro is the most elegant underground railway system in the world. There are 100 stations, many of which are beautifully designed and decorated. There is no graffiti and the stations and trains are quite clean, despite the millions of people travelling along the 203 kilometres of track each day.

Heavy industries
Manufacturing plants, like this factory which makes lorries and tractors, are located in the major industrial regions in the west of what was once the USSR. The heavy industries produce one fifth of the world's total industrial output. Raw materials are abundant: the former USSR had half the world's iron ore reserves and produced more steel than any other country. Since large areas of arid land have now been irrigated, making it possible to grow extra crops, there is a great demand for agricultural machinery.

FORMER SOVIET REPUBLICS

1. GYRFALCON
2. WOLVERINE
3. EUROPEAN BISON

Republic (Capital)	Area sq. km.	(sq. miles)	Population
1. Armenia (Yerevan)	29,800	(11,506)	3,809,000
2. Azerbaijan (Baku)	86,800	(33,436)	7,983,000
3. Belarus (Minsk)	207,976	(80,300)	10,032,000
4. Estonia (Tallinn)	45,099	(17,413)	1,442,000
5. Georgia (Tbilisi)	69,700	(26,911)	5,452,000
6. Kazakhstan (Astana)	2,717,300	(1,049,155)	14,927,000
7. Kyrgyzstan (Bishkek)	198,500	(76,640)	4,865,000
8. Latvia (Riga)	63,959	(24,695)	2,431,000
9. Lithuania (Vilnius)	67,787	(26,173)	3,699,000
10. Moldova (Chişinău)	33,700	(13,012)	4,281,000
11. Russia (Moscow)	17,076,811	(6,593,391)	146,195,000
12. Tajikistan (Dushanbe)	143,100	(55,250)	6,237,000
13. Turkmenistan (Ashgabat)	488,100	(188,455)	4,779,000
14. Ukraine (Kiev)	652,796	(252,046)	49,950,000
15. Uzbekistan (Toshkent)	447,400	(172,740)	24,406,000

Russian ballet

Members of the Bolshoi Ballet performing *Giselle*. Russian ballet is world famous and steeped in tradition. Some of the world's greatest ballets have come from Russia including works such as *Swan Lake*, *The Nutcracker* and *Sleeping Beauty*. The country has also produced some of the world's best dancers, such as Anna Pavlova and Rudolf Nureyev. Both the Bolshoi, based in Moscow, and the Kirov Ballet from St. Petersburg are among the world's best companies.

Shopping in a bazaar

Shopping scenes like this bazaar are a common sight in the new Central Asian republics. Open bazaars sell all kinds of items from bowls and baskets to lamps and rugs.

People also shop in open markets where surplus homegrown produce is sold. These are very popular; the food is fresher, though the price is often higher than in the shops.

As the old Soviet economy collapsed, supplies of food became erratic — commodities in abundance one day became scarce on other occasions, sometimes for long periods.

NORTH AMERICA

North America stretches from the Arctic icecap to the tropical shores of the Caribbean Sea. It includes two of the largest countries in the world, the United States and Canada, and some of the smallest, the tiny island nations of the Caribbean. From Vancouver to St. John's, Newfoundland, the continent measures 5000 kilometres across.

The immensely varied landscape includes the tundra and forests of northern Canada, the vast, featureless croplands of the American Midwest, the deserts of northern Mexico and the rainforests of Central America. Running the length of its western side is North America's mountainous backbone. In this region lie the spectacular peaks of the Rocky Mountains, the Grand Canyon and, in Central America, the active volcanoes of Guatemala, El Salvador and Nicaragua.

The Niagara Falls, which lie between Lake Erie and Lake Ontario.

North America
Highest point Mount McKinley (Alaska, USA) 6194m. (20,320ft.)
Lowest point Death Valley (California, USA) 86m. (282ft.)

Longest river Mississippi-Missouri-Red Rock (USA) 6212 km. (3860 miles)
Largest lake Superior (USA/Canada) 82,348 sq. km. (31,795 sq. miles).

UNITED STATES OF AMERICA
Area 9,372,570 sq. km. (3,618,700 sq. miles)
Population 278,230,000
Capital Washington DC (pop. 523,000)
Largest cities New York City (7,323,000)
Los Angeles (3,485,000)
Chicago (2,784,000)
Houston (1,638,000)
Philadelphia (1,585,000)
Phoenix (988,000)
San Antonio (959,000)
San Diego (1,110,000)
Currency US dollar
Official language(s) English (Spanish is also spoken)
Chief products Wheat, maize, soya beans, minerals, machinery, oil, natural gas, iron and steel
Exports Machinery, vehicles, cereals, chemicals, crude materials
Imports Machinery, vehicles, manufactured goods, food (fish and vegetables), oil

CANADA
Area 9,976,139 sq. km. (3,851,810 sq. miles)
Population 30,491,000
Capital Ottawa-Hull (pop. 1,010,000)
Largest cities Toronto (4,264,000)
Montreal (3,326,000)
Vancouver (1,831,000)
Edmonton (862,000)
Calgary (822,000)
Currency Canadian dollar
Official language(s) English and French
Chief products Wheat, minerals, furs, timber, fish, oil, natural gas
Exports Machinery, paper, vehicles, timber, metals (especially aluminium, nickel, uranium)
Imports Machinery, food, vehicles, chemicals, iron and steel, oil

GREENLAND (Denmark)
Area 2,175,601 sq. km. (840,004 sq. miles)
Population 56,000
Capital Nunk

MEXICO
Official name Estados Unidos Mexicanos
Area 1,972,547 sq. km. (761,610 sq. miles)
Population 96,586,000
Capital Mexico City (pop. 16,674,000)
Largest cities Guadalajara (3,462,000)
Monterrey (3,022,000)
Puebla (1,561,000)
León (1,174,000)
Toluca de Lerdo (1,080,000)
Currency Mexican peso
Official language(s) Spanish (Amerindian languages are also spoken)
Chief products Oil, iron and steel, minerals (especially gold and silver), maize, sorghum, oranges
Exports Oil, manufactured goods, machinery, minerals, textiles, coffee
Imports Vehicles, industrial machinery (motor pumps, textile machinery), food (maize and soya beans)

GUATEMALA
Area 108,889 sq. km. (42,040 sq. miles)
Population 11,088,000
Capital Guatemala City
Chief products Coffee, cotton, chemicals, bananas, maize, sugar cane

NICARAGUA
Area 148,000 sq. km. (57,130 sq. miles)
Population 4,919,000
Capital Managua
Chief products Coffee, cotton, sugar, shellfish

EL SALVADOR
Area 21,041 sq. km. (8120 sq. miles)
Population 6,154,000
Capital San Salvador
Chief products Coffee, textiles, sugar cane, maize

COSTA RICA
Area 50,700 sq. km. (19,600 sq. miles)
Population 3,589,000
Capital San José
Chief products Coffee, bananas, sugar, cocoa, cattle, manufactured goods

Name	Area sq. km. (sq. miles)	Population	Capital	
Anguilla (UK)	91 (35)	10,600	The Valley	
Antigua and Barbuda	442 (171)	67,000	St. John's	
Aruba (Netherlands)	193 (75)	98,000	Oranjestad	
Bahamas	13,864 (5353)	298,000	Nassau	
Barbados	430 (166)	267,000	Bridgetown	
Bermuda (UK)	54 (21)	64,000	Hamilton	
British Virgin Islands (UK)	153 (59)	20,000	Road Town	
Cayman Islands (UK)	259 (100)	39,000	Georgetown	
Dominica	752 (290)	73,000	Roseau	
Grenada	345 (133)	97,000	St. George's	
Guadeloupe (Fr.)	1702 (657)	425,000	Basse-Terre	
Martinique (Fr.)	1079 (417)	384,000	Fort-de-France	
Montserrat (UK)	106 (41)	4000	Plymouth	
Netherlands Antilles (Netherlands)	993 (383)	215,000	Willemstad	
St. Christopher (Kitts)-Nevis	262 (101)	41,000	Basseterre	
St. Lucia	616 (238)	154,000	Castries	
St. Vincent and the Grenadines	388 (150)	114,000	Kingstown	
Trinidad and Tobago	5130 (1980)	1,293,000	Port of Spain	
Turks and Caicos Is. (UK)	430 (192)	17,000	Coburn Town	
US Virgin Islands (USA)	345 (133)	120,000	Charlotte Amalie	
St. Pierre et Miquelon (Fr.)	241 (93)	7000	St. Pierre	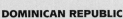

ANTIGUA AND BARBUDA

BAHAMAS

BARBADOS

DOMINICA

GRENADA

ST. CHRISTOPHER (KITTS)-NEVIS

ST. LUCIA

ST. VINCENT AND THE GRENADINES

TRINIDAD AND TOBAGO

US VIRGIN ISLANDS

Note: Countries not marked on the map below appear on the map on page 63.

JAMAICA
Area 10,991 sq. km. (4240 sq. miles)
Population 2,598,000
Capital Kingston
Chief products Sugar, bananas, alumina, bauxite

HAITI
Area 27,750 sq. km. (10,710 sq. miles)
Population 7,803,000
Capital Port-au-Prince
Chief products Coffee, sisal manufactured goods, sugar

DOMINICAN REPUBLIC
Area 48,374 sq. km. (18,820 sq. miles)
Population 8,404,000
Capital Santo Domingo
Chief products Sugar, bauxite, silver, cocoa, coffee

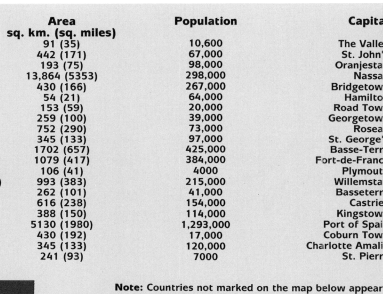

Greenland (Denmark)

Alaska (U.S.)

BELIZE
Area 22,963 sq. km. (8,870 sq. miles)
Population 247,000
Capital Belmopan
Chief products Fruit, fish, vegetables, shellfish, timber

C A N A D A

SAINT PIERRE ET MIQUELON (Fr.)

PUERTO RICO (USA)
Area 9104 sq. km. (3520 sq. miles)
Population 3,890,000
Capital San Juan
Chief products Manufactured goods, sugar cane, machinery, coffee

HONDURAS
Area 112,088 sq. km. (43,280 sq. miles)
Population 6,318,000
Capital Tegucigalpa
Chief products Bananas, coffee, timber, sugar, tobacco

UNITED STATES OF AMERICA

BERMUDA (UK)

CUBA
Area 110,861 sq. km. (42,800 sq. miles)
Population 11,178,000
Capital Havana
Chief products Sugar, oil, minerals (nickel, iron ore), rice, maize, coffee, tobacco

PANAMA
Area 77,082 sq. km. (29,670 sq. miles)
Population 2,811,000
Capital Panamá
Chief products Bananas, timber, copper, rice, sugar

MEXICO

BAHAMAS
CUBA
PUERTO RICO (US)
ANTIGUA & BARBUDA
DOMINICAN REPUBLIC
HAITI
DOMINICA
JAMAICA
ST. LUCIA
ST. VINCENT
GRENADA
BARBADOS
TRINIDAD & TOBAGO
BELIZE
GUATEMALA HONDURAS
EL SALVADOR NICARAGUA
PANAMA
COSTA RICA

CANADA

anada is the second largest country in the world, yet eighty-nine per cent of the land has no permanent population. Much of Canada's territory is either tundra (Arctic plains where the subsoil is permanently frozen) or forest. Most of the people live in the urban areas by the Great Lakes and the St. Lawrence Seaway, a major shipping route.

Canada has rich natural resources of minerals such as zinc, nickel and uranium. Pulp and paper are made from the huge supplies of wood, while vast prairie lands make Canada one of the world's leading producers of wheat. Deep-sea fishing is important on the Atlantic coast of Canada: shellfish, lobster and cod are canned or frozen for export.

The Welland Canal
The Welland canal connects two of the Great Lakes, Erie and Ontario.

It is deep enough for container ships, bound for the Atlantic Ocean via the St. Lawrence Seaway.

The Prairies
The plains of Alberta, Saskatchewan and Manitoba in central Canada are known as the Prairies.

54

BEAUFORT
SEA

Banks
Island

Dawson

YUKON
TERRITORY

Mackenzie Mountains

Mackenzie

Great
Bear Lake

Mt Logan
6050

Yukon

N O R T H W E S

T E R R I T O R I

Whitehorse

C

A

Yellowkn

Rocky

Queen
Charlotte
Islands

B R I T I S H

A L B E R

Prince George

C O L U M B I A

Edmonto

Coast

Mountains

Mountains

Vancouver I.

Fraser

Calgary

Vancouver

Victoria

Pe

Ice hockey
Ice hockey is Canada's national game. In winter it is played outside and every district has a boys' and a girls' hockey league.

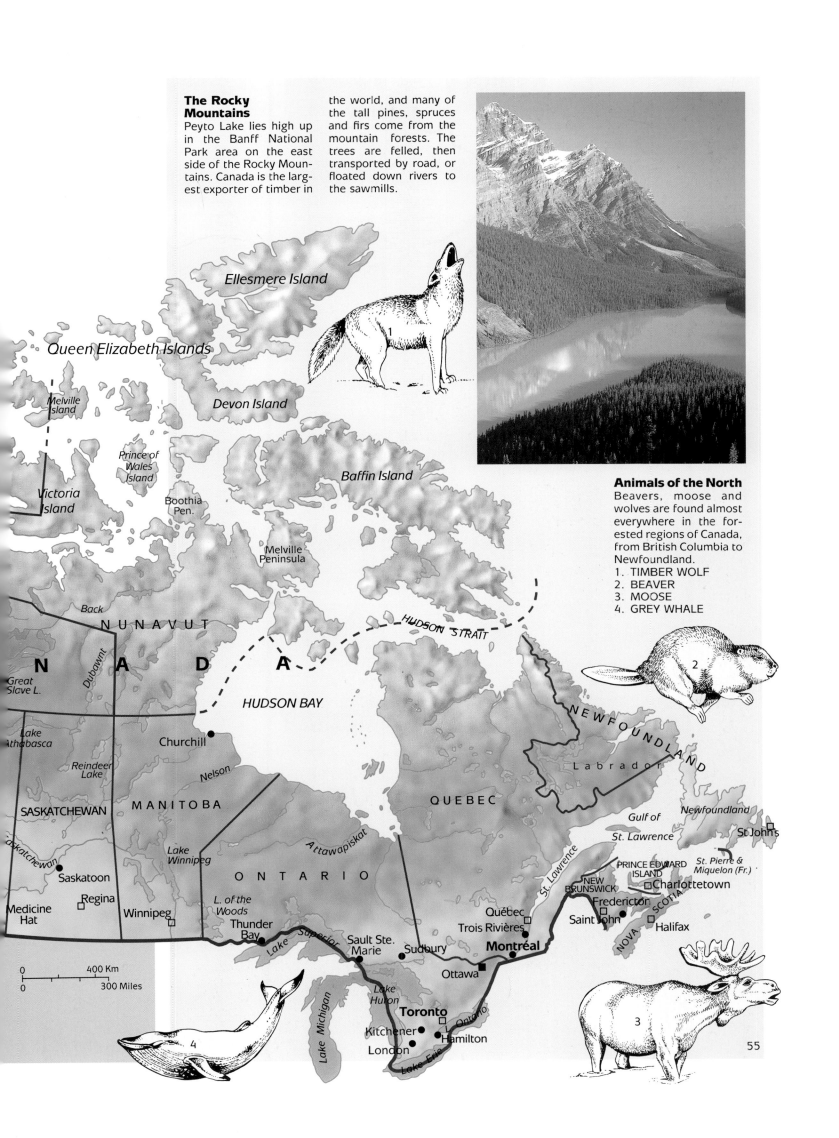

The Rocky Mountains

Peyto Lake lies high up in the Banff National Park area on the east side of the Rocky Mountains. Canada is the largest exporter of timber in the world, and many of the tall pines, spruces and firs come from the mountain forests. The trees are felled, then transported by road, or floated down rivers to the sawmills.

Animals of the North

Beavers, moose and wolves are found almost everywhere in the forested regions of Canada, from British Columbia to Newfoundland.
1. TIMBER WOLF
2. BEAVER
3. MOOSE
4. GREY WHALE

Ellesmere Island

Queen Elizabeth Islands

Melville Island

Prince of Wales Island

Victoria Island

Devon Island

Boothia Pen.

Baffin Island

Melville Peninsula

Back

NUNAVUT

N A N A D A

Dubawnt

Great Slave L.

Lake Athabasca

Reindeer Lake

Churchill

Nelson

HUDSON STRAIT

HUDSON BAY

NEWFOUNDLAND

Labrador

SASKATCHEWAN

MANITOBA

Saskatchewan

Saskatoon

Lake Winnipeg

Attawapiskat

QUEBEC

Gulf of St. Lawrence

Newfoundland

St John's

Medicine Hat

Regina

Winnipeg

ONTARIO

L. of the Woods

Thunder Bay

Lake Superior

Sault Ste. Marie

Sudbury

St. Lawrence

PRINCE EDWARD ISLAND

NEW BRUNSWICK

St. Pierre & Miquelon (Fr.)

Charlottetown

Fredericton

Québec

Trois Rivières

Montréal

Ottawa

Saint John

NOVA SCOTIA

Halifax

Lake Michigan

Lake Huron

Toronto

Lake Ontario

Kitchener

London

Hamilton

Lake Erie

0   400 Km
0   300 Miles

55

UNITED STATES OF AMERICA

The United States of America is the fourth largest country in the world. It is made up of 50 states, 48 of which lie between Canada and Mexico. The other two are the islands of Hawaii in the Pacific Ocean, and Alaska in the north-western corner of North America, which was bought from the Russians in 1867.

The USA is a country of enormous natural resources. Between the Rocky Mountains in the west and the Appalachian Mountains in the east lie vast areas of prairie land where maize, wheat, soya beans and many other crops are grown on highly-mechanized farms. Despite large reserves of oil in Alaska, the USA is such a huge consumer that it still has to import stocks of oil.

cont. page 58

Bryce Canyon, Utah
Bryce Canyon is about 150 kilometres north of the Grand Canyon. Centuries of erosion from wind and frost have produced this spectacle of brilliantly coloured spires. The canyon is a large U-shaped amphitheatre, one and a half kilometres wide.

Wildlife in the USA
Three animals from the great variety of wildlife in the USA.
1. CALIFORNIA SEALION
2. RACCOON
3. BALD EAGLE

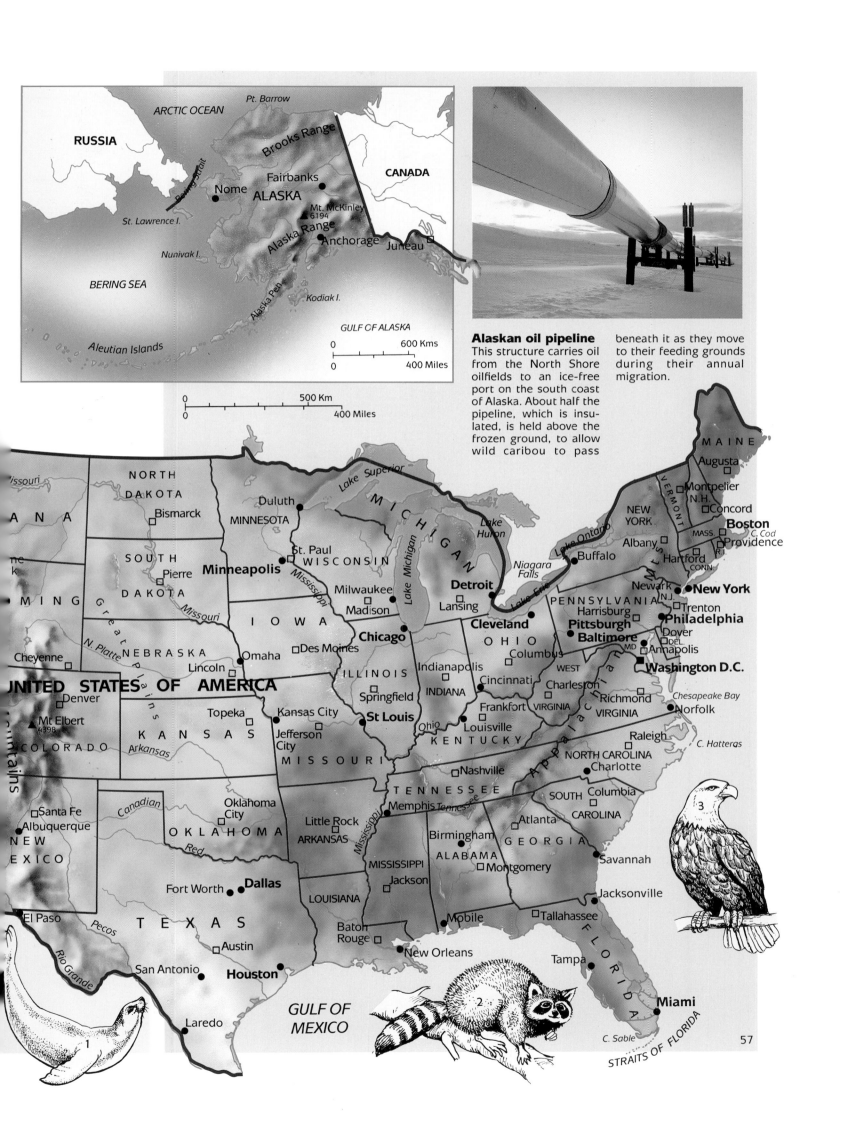

Alaskan oil pipeline
This structure carries oil from the North Shore oilfields to an ice-free port on the south coast of Alaska. About half the pipeline, which is insulated, is held above the frozen ground, to allow wild caribou to pass beneath it as they move to their feeding grounds during their annual migration.

Heavy industry is concentrated in the north-east and around the Great Lakes, but more recently high-tech and light industry has developed in the west, especially in California, which is now the biggest manufacturing state in the USA.

People have come from every continent to live in the USA. The early European settlers learned much about their new home from the native Americans. While most immigrants came in search of a better life, black people were brought over by force from West Africa to work as slaves on Southern plantations. Huge numbers of European immigrants arrived in the late nineteenth century, followed by waves of new-comers from Asia and Latin America in this century.

The USA is famous for many things: its space technology which put the first man on the moon; New York City with its skyscrapers and important financial centre; the film industry in Hollywood; and the beautiful national parks, such as the Grand Canyon and Yellowstone.

Navajo Indians
Many Indians live in areas set aside for them called reservations. The Navajo reservation in the south-west is the largest.

Farming in Southern California
These men are loading lettuces on to a truck. California, on the west coast of the USA, sells more farm products than any other state. Particular areas of California specialize in particular crops – citrus fruits and vines are cultivated in central California.

Pittsburgh (top)
Pittsburgh is one of the centres of heavy manu-facturing in the northern USA with large iron and steel and chemical works.

58

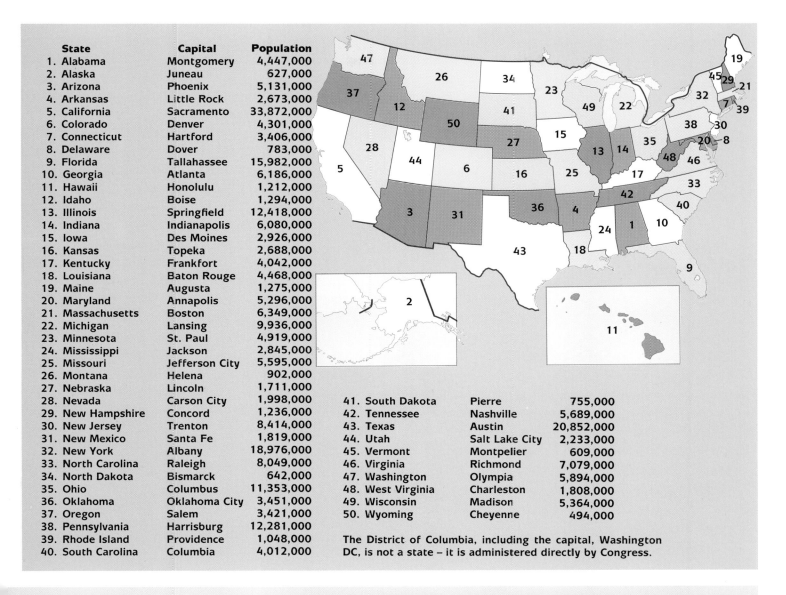

	State	Capital	Population
1.	Alabama	Montgomery	4,447,000
2.	Alaska	Juneau	627,000
3.	Arizona	Phoenix	5,131,000
4.	Arkansas	Little Rock	2,673,000
5.	California	Sacramento	33,872,000
6.	Colorado	Denver	4,301,000
7.	Connecticut	Hartford	3,406,000
8.	Delaware	Dover	783,000
9.	Florida	Tallahassee	15,982,000
10.	Georgia	Atlanta	6,186,000
11.	Hawaii	Honolulu	1,212,000
12.	Idaho	Boise	1,294,000
13.	Illinois	Springfield	12,418,000
14.	Indiana	Indianapolis	6,080,000
15.	Iowa	Des Moines	2,926,000
16.	Kansas	Topeka	2,688,000
17.	Kentucky	Frankfort	4,042,000
18.	Louisiana	Baton Rouge	4,468,000
19.	Maine	Augusta	1,275,000
20.	Maryland	Annapolis	5,296,000
21.	Massachusetts	Boston	6,349,000
22.	Michigan	Lansing	9,936,000
23.	Minnesota	St. Paul	4,919,000
24.	Mississippi	Jackson	2,845,000
25.	Missouri	Jefferson City	5,595,000
26.	Montana	Helena	902,000
27.	Nebraska	Lincoln	1,711,000
28.	Nevada	Carson City	1,998,000
29.	New Hampshire	Concord	1,236,000
30.	New Jersey	Trenton	8,414,000
31.	New Mexico	Santa Fe	1,819,000
32.	New York	Albany	18,976,000
33.	North Carolina	Raleigh	8,049,000
34.	North Dakota	Bismarck	642,000
35.	Ohio	Columbus	11,353,000
36.	Oklahoma	Oklahoma City	3,451,000
37.	Oregon	Salem	3,421,000
38.	Pennsylvania	Harrisburg	12,281,000
39.	Rhode Island	Providence	1,048,000
40.	South Carolina	Columbia	4,012,000
41.	South Dakota	Pierre	755,000
42.	Tennessee	Nashville	5,689,000
43.	Texas	Austin	20,852,000
44.	Utah	Salt Lake City	2,233,000
45.	Vermont	Montpelier	609,000
46.	Virginia	Richmond	7,079,000
47.	Washington	Olympia	5,894,000
48.	West Virginia	Charleston	1,808,000
49.	Wisconsin	Madison	5,364,000
50.	Wyoming	Cheyenne	494,000

The District of Columbia, including the capital, Washington DC, is not a state – it is administered directly by Congress.

Jazz band, New Orleans

The first jazz bands started in the city of New Orleans in the South. The 'Great Age' of jazz was in the 1920s when New Orleans was a colourful and cosmopolitan city. Groups of black musicians would play together spontaneously and new styles of dancing developed. Much of today's pop music originated from jazz.

New Hampshire in the autumn

The far north-eastern corner of the USA, known as New England, is renowned for the colours of the leaves in autumn. Outdoor sports such as fishing, hunting and skiing are very popular in the unspoilt countryside. This is where the Pilgrims from Britain settled in the early seventeenth century, and many of the place names are derived from towns and villages in England.

CENTRAL AMERICA AND MEXICO

Mexico and the Central American countries – Guatemala, Nicaragua, El Salvador, Honduras, Belize, Costa Rica and Panama – form a long land bridge joining North and South America. The Pacific Ocean lies to the west; the Gulf of Mexico to the east. Mexico is the largest of these countries – in fact more people live in its capital, Mexico City, than in any of the other Central American states.

The people of Mexico and Central America are descended from the original Indian tribes that inhabited the area, and from the Spanish who arrived in the sixteenth century. Many people are of mixed Indian and Spanish blood and are known as *mestizos*.

Mexico has valuable natural reserves of gold and silver, and large oil fields in the Gulf of Mexico. The economies of the Central American countries rely heavily on the export of crops such as cotton, bananas and sugar.

A market in Xochimilco, Mexico
This woman is weaving a traditional rug at a market. Hand-weaving is an ancient Indian art that is still practised, especially in the south where there is a larger native Indian population. Styles vary according to region so that the region which an Indian comes from can be identified by the colours and patterns on their clothes and rugs.

Cacti in the Mexican desert

The cactus plant is often the only form of life in the deserts of northern Mexico. Some years there is no rain at all, especially in Lower California. However, there are hundreds of different species of cacti, and some yield juices which are turned into alcoholic drinks. One of these drinks is called tequila which is used to make cocktails. Plantations are now run to produce tequila for export, as it has become popular around the world. A stronger and cheaper drink, which has been made since the days of the Mayans, is pulque, known as the poor Mexican's beer. The juice is squeezed from the fleshy leaves of a very tall variety of cactus, often taller than a person.

The Panama Canal

The Panama Canal is one of the greatest feats of engineering in the world. It is 65 kilometres long, and was built so that ships could pass between the Atlantic and Pacific Oceans without having to sail south round South America. This involved hacking out kilometres of rock, damming rivers and building huge iron locks. It was completed by the USA but a 1978 treaty provides for its gradual takeover by Panama. The canal is very important to world trade, and shipping companies have to pay a high toll to the Panamanian government for its use. The canal provides many jobs for the local people.

Cutting bananas

The banana is one of the most important crops grown in the countries of Central America. Machete knives are used to cut the clumps of bananas while they are still green. They are then exported to the USA and Europe in time for them to ripen just before delivery to the shops.

Map labels

uahua
Río Grande
Nuevo Laredo
Sierra Madre Oriental
M É X I C O
Torreón
Saltillo
Matamoros
Monterrey
GULF OF MEXICO
idental
San Luis Potosí
Tampico
Grande de Santiago
Aguascalientes
León
Querétaro
dalajara
Morelia
Mexico City
Veracruz
Gulf of Campeche
Mérida
I. de Cozumel
Yucatán
Cuernavaca
Puebla
Citlaltepetl 5700
Balsas
Orizaba
Acapulco
Minatitlán
Isthmus of Tehuantepec
Belmopan
Belize City
BELIZE
Oaxaca
Gulf of Tehuantepec
GUATEMALA
Guatemala City
HONDURAS
C. Gracias á Dios
Tegucigalpa
San Salvador
EL SALVADOR
Mosquito Coast
NICARAGUA
PACIFIC OCEAN
Managua
L. Nicaragua
COSTA RICA
San José
Panama Canal
Panamá
PANAMA
Gulf of Panama

0   500 Km
0   400 Miles

CARIBBEAN ISLANDS

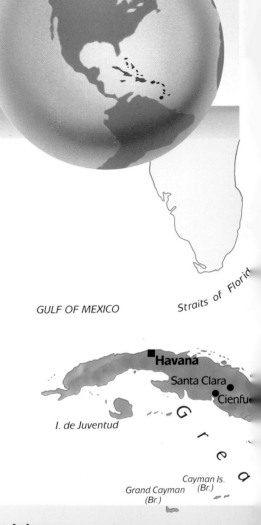

The islands of the West Indies lie between North and South America. Commonly known as the Caribbean, this region contains fourteen countries, scattered over many islands, whose populations range in size from a few thousand to over eleven million, and whose people speak four main languages.

Today over half of the countries of the Caribbean are politically independent; others, such as the British Virgin Islands and Guadeloupe, are still possessions. The wealth of the Caribbean countries varies immensely. Puerto Rico has a well-developed industrial base. Many of the islands have thriving tourist industries. In contrast, Haiti is one of the poorest countries in the western hemisphere.

The tropical climate of this region is especially suited to growing sugar cane, which is used to produce sugar, molasses (a kind of syrup) and rum for export. Other crops include coffee, tobacco, cacao (to make chocolate and cocoa) and citrus fruits.

GULF OF MEXICO

Straits of Florida

Havana

Santa Clara

Cienfu

I. de Juventud

Cayman Is.
Grand Cayman   (Br.)
(Br.)

Cutting sugar cane in Cuba

Sugar cane is Cuba's most valuable crop. It makes up seventy-five per cent of its exports. Long knives called machetes are used to cut down the cane, which is then taken to the sugar mills for processing. The cane is ground in the mill and boiled in water until sugar crystals are formed. If the cane is first fermented, it can be distilled into rum.

Festival time

Music can be heard everywhere at carnival time in the Caribbean. People dress in traditional costumes and dance in the streets. Reggae music from Jamaica and calypso songs from Trinidad are especially popular. The musical instruments include drums made from hollow logs, and shakers from dried gourds.

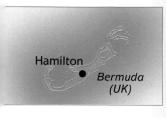

Hamilton
Bermuda
(UK)

Curaçao

Many of the Caribbean islands show the influence of the European settlers in the past. Curaçao was first occupied by the Spanish and then by the Dutch. Many of its buildings today – churches, halls, schools and houses – were erected by the colonists. The main language spoken on Curaçao is Dutch. Also spoken is a patois that developed from the earliest contacts between Europeans and Africans who were brought to the island as slaves.

Bartering for fish

Fish is often sold straight from the boat in the Caribbean. Local fishers sail up the busy quayside, where in some places there are floating markets. Everybody gathers round to see the fresh catch and the bartering begins. The people shout out offers for particular pieces of fish, depending on the type and size. There is a rich diversity of fish in the Caribbean Sea and it is an important food of the islands.

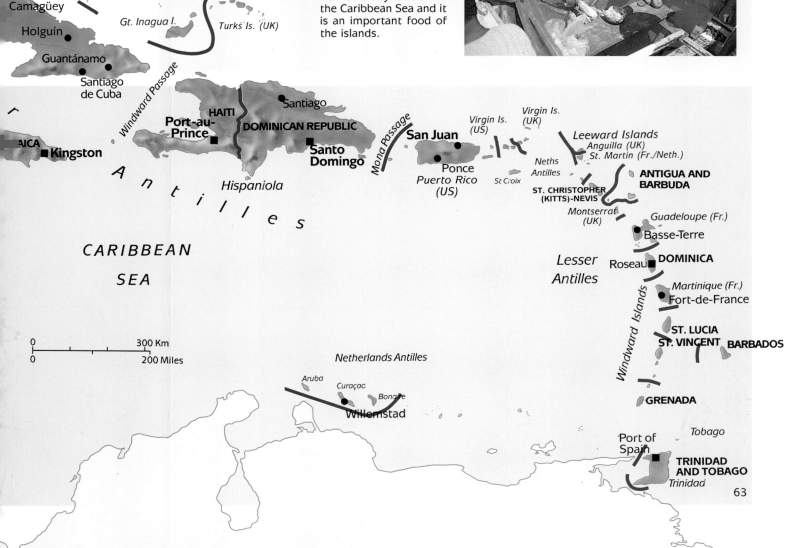

Gt. Abaco I.
na I.
New Providence I.
Eleuthera I.
■ Nassau **BAHAMAS**
Cat. I.
Andros I.
Long I.

CUBA
Camagüey
Acklins I.
Holguín
Gt. Inagua I.
Caicos Is. (UK)
Guantánamo
Turks Is. (UK)
Santiago de Cuba

Windward Passage

A n t i l l e s

AICA ■ Kingston
Santiago
HAITI
Port-au-Prince ■
DOMINICAN REPUBLIC ■
Mona Passage
San Juan ●
Virgin Is. (US)
Virgin Is. (UK)
Santo Domingo
Hispaniola
Ponce ●
Puerto Rico (US)
St Croix
Leeward Islands
Anguilla (UK)
St. Martin (Fr./Neth.)
Neths Antilles
ST. CHRISTOPHER (KITTS)-NEVIS
ANTIGUA AND BARBUDA
Montserrat (UK)
Guadeloupe (Fr.)
● Basse-Terre

CARIBBEAN
SEA
Lesser Antilles
Roseau ■ **DOMINICA**
Martinique (Fr.)
● Fort-de-France

0 — 300 Km
0 — 200 Miles

Netherlands Antilles
Aruba
Curaçac
Bonare
Willemstad

Windward Islands
ST. LUCIA
ST. VINCENT **BARBADOS**

● **GRENADA**

Tobago
Port of Spain ■
TRINIDAD AND TOBAGO
Trinidad

SOUTH AMERICA

South America stretches from the Caribbean Sea down to Cape Horn, the cold southernmost tip which is only 990 kilometres away from Antarctica. It is made up of thirteen countries; the largest is Brazil which covers nearly half of the total area of the continent.

The Andes mountains run almost the entire length of South America, with peaks up to 7000 metres. Spanning the continent, from its source in the Peruvian Andes through the Brazilian rainforest to the Atlantic Ocean, is the river Amazon, at 6515 kilometres the second longest river in the world. South of the rainforest are the plateau grasslands of the Pampas. To the west of the Andes, squeezed between the coast and the mountains, lies the Atacama Desert, reputedly the driest desert in the world.

The Straits of Magellan in southern Chile.

South America
Highest point Mount Aconcagua (Argentina) 6960m. (22,834ft.) above sea level
Lowest point Peninsula Valdés (Argentina) 40m. (131ft.) below sea level
Longest river Amazon 6515km. (4050 miles)
Largest lake Titicaca (Peru/Bolivia) 8340 sq. km. (3220 sq. miles)

ARGENTINA
Official name República Argentina
Area 2,766,889 sq. km. (1,068,302 sq. miles)
Population 36,580,000
Capital Buenos Aires (pop. 14,400,000)
Largest cities Córdoba (1,275,000)
Rosario (1,000,000)
Tucumán (622,000)
La Plata (576,000)
Mar de Plata (579,000)
Santa Fé (406,000)
Currency Peso
Official language(s) Spanish
Chief products Meat products (especially beef and mutton), wool, oil, minerals (coal, lead, zinc and iron ore), natural gas, wine, machine tools, vehicles, textiles, wheat, maize
Exports Meat, cereals, wool
Imports Machinery, iron and steel, non-ferrous metals

BRAZIL
Official name República Federativa do Brasil
Area 8,511,965 sq. km. (3,286,488 sq. miles)
Population 167,967,000
Capital Brasilia (pop. 1,821,000)
Largest cities São Paulo (16,583,000)
Rio de Janeiro (5,552,000)
Salvador (2,221,000)
Belo Horizonte (2,091,000)
Fortaleza (1,965,000)
Curitíba (1,476,000)
Currency Real
Official language(s) Portuguese (Italian, Spanish, German, Japanese, Arabic are also spoken)
Chief products Iron ore, manganese, bauxite, chrome, diamonds, maize, black beans, cassava, coffee, cotton, soya, rice
Exports Coffee, cotton, iron ore, machinery
Imports Machinery, crude oil, cereals, non-ferrous metals

BOLIVIA
Official name República de Bolivia
Area 1,098,581 sq. km. (424,164 sq. miles)
Population 8,138,000
Capital La Paz (Legal capital – Sucre)
Official language(s) Spanish
Chief products Tin, natural gas, coffee, wood, natural rubber, potatoes, maize

CHILE
Official name República de Chile
Area 756,626 sq. km. (292,132 sq. miles)
Population 15,018,000
Capital Santiago
Official language(s) Spanish
Chief products Copper, nitrate, wheat, livestock, fish, iron ore, timber, vegetables, fruit, silver

COLOMBIA
Official name República de Colombia
Area 1,141,748 sq. km. (440,831 sq. miles)
Population 41,539,000
Capital Bogotá
Official language(s) Spanish
Chief products Coffee, cotton, bananas, tobacco, gold, coal, oil, textiles, precious stones

ECUADOR
Official name República del Ecuador
Area 461,475 sq. km. (178,130 sq. miles)
Population 12,412,000
Capital Quito
Official language(s) Spanish
Chief products Bananas, coffee, cocoa, oil, rice, fish (especially shrimps and sardines), African palm

Beautiful scenery high
in the Andes.

PERU
Official name República
del Perú
Area 1,285,216 sq. km.
(496,225 sq. miles)
Population 25,230,000
Capital Lima (pop. 6,465,000)
Largest cities Arequipa
(619,000)
Trujillo (532,000)
Chiclayo (426,000)
Currency Nuevo Sol
Official language(s)
Spanish and Quechua
Chief products Fishmeal,
iron ore, copper, silver, zinc,
lead, sugar, wheat, maize,
oil, timber, cotton

VENEZUELA
Official name República
de Venezuela
Area 912,050 sq. km.
(352,144 sq. miles)
Population 23,707,000
Capital Caracas
Official language(s)
Spanish
Chief products Oil,
petro-chemicals,
aluminium, plastics, steel
products, gold, diamonds,
asbestos, textiles

GUYANA
Official name The
Co-operative Republic of
Guyana
Area 214,969 sq. km.
(83,000 sq. miles)
Population 856,000
Capital Georgetown
Official language(s)
English
Chief products Sugar,
rice, bauxite, alumina,
diamonds, gold, timber,
rum

PARAGUAY
Official name República
del Paraguay
Area 406,752 sq. km.
(157,042 sq. miles)
Population 5,359,000
Capital Asunción
Official language(s)
Spanish (Guarini is also
spoken)
Chief products Processed
meat, cotton, soya beans,
tobacco, sugar, coffee,
timber

URUGUAY
Official name República
Oriental del Uruguay
Area 176,215 sq. km.
(68,037 sq. miles)
Population 3,313,000
Capital Montevideo
Official language(s)
Spanish
Chief products Wool,
meat products, textiles,
fish, fruits, wheat, barley,
maize, oil products

SURINAM
Official name Nieuwe
Republiek van Suriname
Area 163,265 sq. km.
(63,037 sq. miles)
Population 413,000
Capital Paramaribo
Official language(s)
Dutch (English and Sranan
Tongo are also spoken)
Chief products Timber,
rice, sugar cane, bauxite

**FALKLAND ISLANDS
(UK)**
Area 12,175 sq. km.
(4700 sq. miles)
Population 2500
Capital Port Stanley

FRENCH GUIANA
Official name Guyane
Française
Area 88,533 sq. km.
(32,252 sq. miles)
Population 159,000
Capital Cayenne
Official language(s)
French (Creole is also
spoken)
Chief products Fish
(especially shrimps),
timber, cayenne pepper

NORTHERN SOUTH AMERICA

The landscape of the countries of this region varies from the mountain ranges and plains of the Andes mountains in the west to the tropical rainforests of the north.

Many of the countries have rich mineral resources. Venezuela is a leading producer of oil; Colombia mines emeralds, gold and coal, and is a major exporter of coffee. Silver, zinc, iron and tin have all been discovered in the mountainous areas of Bolivia and Peru. Agriculture varies from the subsistence farming practised by the Bolivian Indians on the high plateau around Lake Titicaca to the high levels of production of a country such as Ecuador, which is a leading exporter of bananas.

The people of these countries are descended from the native Indians and the European settlers who conquered the region in the sixteenth century. In Peru and Bolivia over half the people are of Indian blood, speaking the original Inca language, Quechua, and Aymara.

Lake Titicaca
Outside their reed home on Lake Titicaca, these women are making clothes to be sold at market. Lake Titicaca lies between Peru and Bolivia and is the highest lake in the world.

Life in the Andes
In the south-west of Bolivia lies part of the high Andes mountain range. In this region the average yearly temperature is as low as four degrees Celsius. At these high altitudes no trees can survive, and it is too cold to grow crops. The Bolivian people who inhabit this area live by herding llamas, the hardy animals pictured above which are kept for their wool and meat.

66

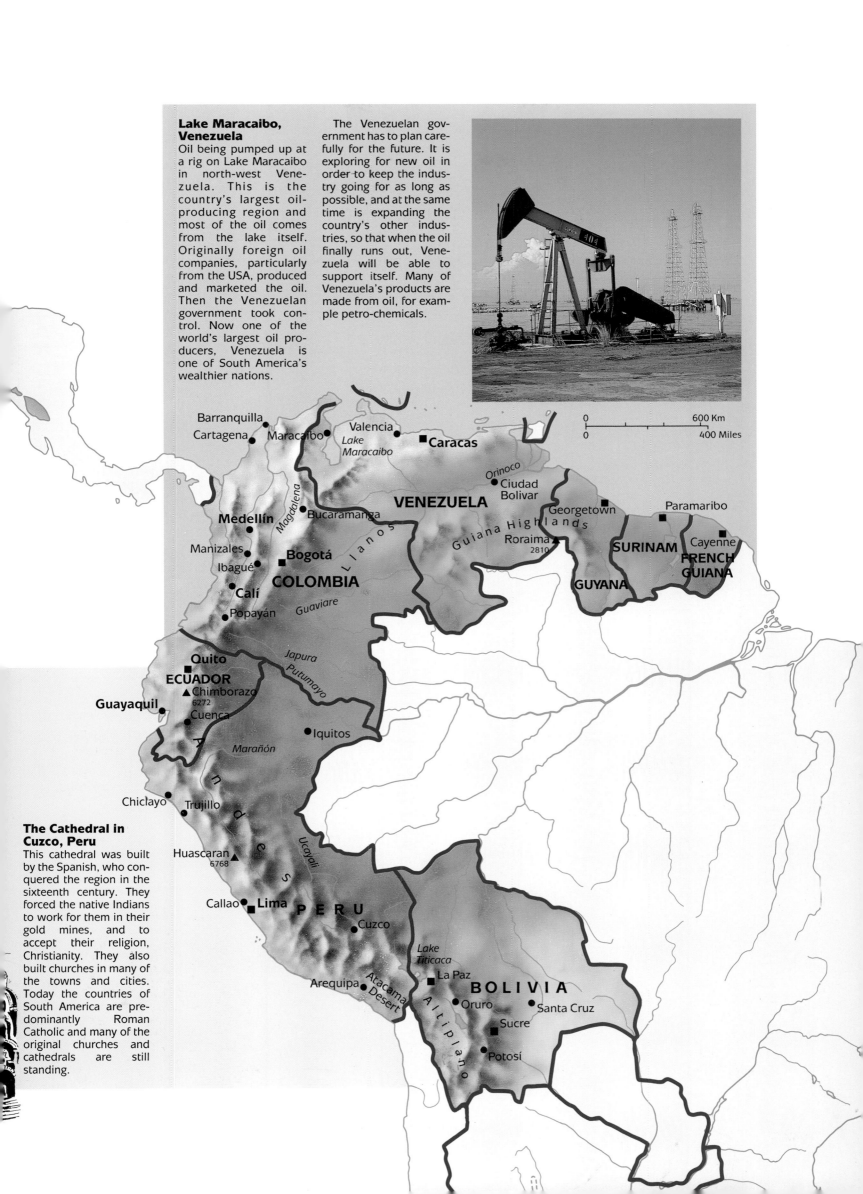

Lake Maracaibo, Venezuela

Oil being pumped up at a rig on Lake Maracaibo in north-west Venezuela. This is the country's largest oil-producing region and most of the oil comes from the lake itself. Originally foreign oil companies, particularly from the USA, produced and marketed the oil. Then the Venezuelan government took control. Now one of the world's largest oil producers, Venezuela is one of South America's wealthier nations.

The Venezuelan government has to plan carefully for the future. It is exploring for new oil in order to keep the industry going for as long as possible, and at the same time is expanding the country's other industries, so that when the oil finally runs out, Venezuela will be able to support itself. Many of Venezuela's products are made from oil, for example petro-chemicals.

The Cathedral in Cuzco, Peru

This cathedral was built by the Spanish, who conquered the region in the sixteenth century. They forced the native Indians to work for them in their gold mines, and to accept their religion, Christianity. They also built churches in many of the towns and cities. Today the countries of South America are predominantly Roman Catholic and many of the original churches and cathedrals are still standing.

0   600 Km
0   400 Miles

Barranquilla
Cartagena
Maracaibo
Valencia
Lake Maracaibo
Caracas

VENEZUELA

Orinoco
Ciudad Bolivar

Georgetown

Paramaribo

Medellín
Bucaramanga
Magdalena

Guiana Highlands

Roraima 2810

SURINAM

Cayenne

Manizales

Bogotá

Ibagué

COLOMBIA

Cali

Popayán

Guaviare

GUYANA

FRENCH GUIANA

Llanos

Japura

Putumayo

Quito

ECUADOR

▲ Chimborazo 6272

Guayaquil

Cuenca

Marañón

Iquitos

Chiclayo
Trujillo

Huascaran ▲ 6768

Andes

Ucayali

Callao **Lima**

P E R U

Cuzco

Lake Titicaca

La Paz

BOLIVIA

Arequipa
Atacama Desert

Oruro
Santa Cruz

Altiplano

Sucre

Potosí

BRAZIL

Brazil is the largest country in South America. For a long time it was governed by Portugal, and Portuguese is still the language spoken by most Brazilians. Brazil is a tropical country and it contains the largest area of tropical rainforest in the world.

The Amazon, the world's second longest river, runs through Brazil. For most of its course it flows through the hot, steamy jungles of the tropical rainforest. In north-east Brazil the climate is dry and farming is difficult, but farther south there are vast grazing lands. Iron ore is mined in the south-east of the country, where coffee and oranges are also produced. These are important exports for Brazil. The main cities are situated in this region. São Paulo is one of South America's most crowded cities, but the beauty of Rio de Janeiro attracts visitors from all over the world. Brazil's capital is Brasilia, a new city that was built so that the government would be situated in the centre of the country.

Rainforest
Clearing away the rainforest in Brazil. Every year developers and timber companies destroy rainforest equal to three times the size of Switzerland. Unknown numbers of plants and animals are being lost, and soils washed away.

Rio de Janeiro
Rio's carnival is famous throughout the world. Every year during Mardi Gras thousands of people dress in spectacular costumes and parade through the streets. For days on end there is singing and dancing to the rhythms of Brazilian music.

Brazil's cities
Many people in Brazil's cities live in very poor conditions. Some live in old houses which are ready to collapse.

0		600 Km
0		400 Miles

68

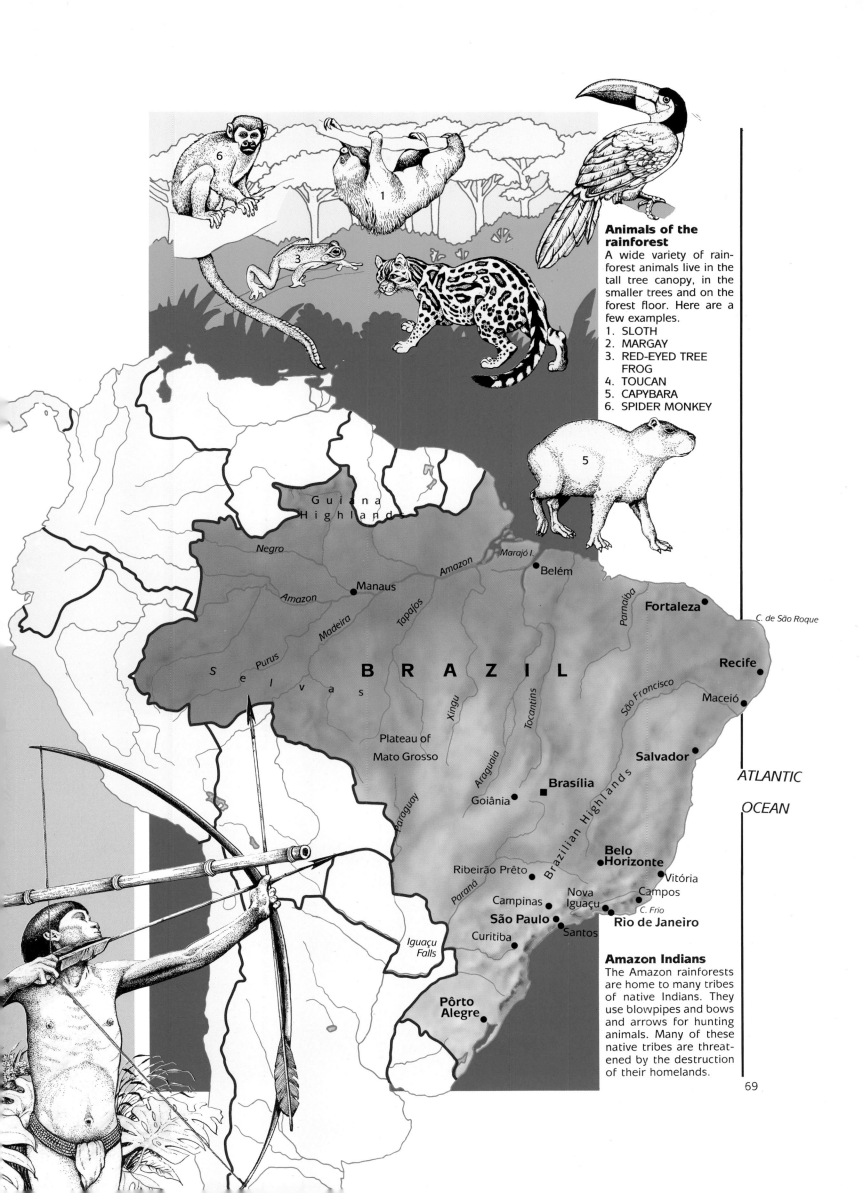

Animals of the rainforest

A wide variety of rainforest animals live in the tall tree canopy, in the smaller trees and on the forest floor. Here are a few examples.

1. SLOTH
2. MARGAY
3. RED-EYED TREE FROG
4. TOUCAN
5. CAPYBARA
6. SPIDER MONKEY

Guiana Highlands

Negro

Amazon

Marajó I.

Belém

Amazon

Manaus

Madeira

Tapajós

Parnaíba

Fortaleza

C. de São Roque

Purus

S e l v a s

B R A Z I L

Recife

São Francisco

Maceió

Xingu

Tocantins

Plateau of Mato Grosso

Araguaia

Salvador

ATLANTIC

Brasília

OCEAN

Paraguay

Goiânia

Brazilian Highlands

Belo Horizonte

Ribeirão Prêto

Paraná

Vitória

Campos

Campinas

Nova Iguaçu

C. Frio

São Paulo

Santos

Rio de Janeiro

Curitiba

Iguaçu Falls

Amazon Indians

The Amazon rainforests are home to many tribes of native Indians. They use blowpipes and bows and arrows for hunting animals. Many of these native tribes are threatened by the destruction of their homelands.

Pôrto Alegre

SOUTHERN SOUTH AMERICA

Like much of the continent, many parts of southern South America were conquered by the Spanish in the sixteenth century. Since then immigrants from many European countries have settled there. Some areas, such as the sub-tropical forests of Paraguay, and the Andes mountains of Chile, still have Indian inhabitants.

Most people live in the large cities: Buenos Aires, the capital of Argentina, is home to one third of Argentina's population, while one half of the people in Uruguay live in its capital, Montevideo. On the vast areas of grassland in Paraguay, Uruguay and Argentina sheep and cattle are grazed, supplying the meat-packing, wool and textile industries. Argentina also produces wheat and maize, grown on fields in the Pampas region. In Patagonia, in the south, there are big reserves of oil and gas. Chile has huge mineral deposits, and is one of the world's largest suppliers of copper, which is found in the Atacama Desert in the northern part of the country.

Gauchos
Gauchos are similar to North American cowboys. Traditionally their main job was to take cattle to the markets in the large towns of Argentina, Paraguay and Uruguay, often riding for several weeks through the grasslands. Today, many of them ride motorbikes and tractors instead of horses.

Chiloé island
The large island of Chiloé lies close to the mainland near Puerto Montt in Chile. The climate is wet and the area prone to earthquakes. The island's port, Castro, was founded in 1567. Many of the houses there are built on stilts in order to raise them clear of soft ground and the floodwater from tidal waves.

Football crazy
Football is the national sport of all the Latin American countries. Uruguay and Argentina have both won the World Cup twice.

The Chilean landscape

Chile, the longest, narrowest country on Earth, is no more than 380 kilometres wide at any point, but is 4265 kilometres long, stretching down South America's west coast between the Andes mountains and the Pacific Ocean.

The south of this country is a landscape of lakes, roaring waterfalls and fuming volcanoes capped with snow, as can be seen in this view of Lake Villarrica. Around Cape Horn, the southernmost tip of South America, lie many thousands of islands and a labyrinth of fjords.

0 — 600 Km
0 — 400 Miles

Atacama Desert

Iquique

Chaco

PARAGUAY

Pilcomayo

Antofagasta

Gran

Asunción

Tucumán

Salado

Paraná

Corrientes

Uruguay

Andes

San Juan

Córdoba
Santa Fe

Salto

URUGUAY

Aconcagua
6960

Mendoza

Rosario

Valparaíso

Santiago

Montevideo

Buenos Aires

La Plata

CHILE

ARGENTINA

Pampas

ATLANTIC OCEAN

Concepción

Colorado

Mar del Plata

Negro

Bahia Blanca

Valdivia

Puerto Montt

Pen.
Valdés

Chiloé I.

Chonos
Arch.

Patagonia

Comodoro Rivadavia

Falkland Islands
(UK)

Port Stanley

Magellan's Strait

Tierra del Fuego

C. Horn

Argentina

In 1816 Argentina declared independence from Spanish rule. Today, it has the second largest population in South America. Its cities are large and cosmopolitan although many of the rural areas are still fairly undeveloped. This picture (*left*) shows the Plaza de la República in the capital of Argentina, Buenos Aires.

ASIA

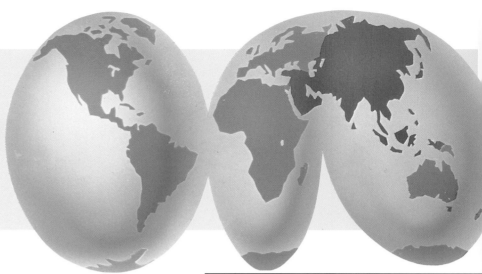

Asia is the largest of the continents and contains more than half of the people on Earth. It has two of the most populous countries in the world: China and India. Many of the most densely populated countries are also in Asia.

The variety of landscape is huge. In northern Russia lies a vast area of coniferous forest, while the desert lands of the Gobi cover much of Mongolia. Farther south lie China's vast cultivated plains, and on the edge of the Pacific Ocean volcanic islands support lush tropical vegetation.

North of the Indian subcontinent, in Nepal and Tibet, the Himalayas and the high Tibetan Plateau form the 'rooftop of the world'. From these icy heights flow the tributaries of some of the great river systems of this region, the Yangtze, Irrawaddy, Mekong, Ganges and Indus rivers. cont. page 74

A high mountain peak in the Himalayas in Nepal.

Asia
Highest point Mount Everest (Nepal/China) 8848m. (29,028ft.)
Lowest point Shore of Dead Sea (Israel/Jordan) 399m. (1310ft.) below sea level.

Longest river Yangtze (China) 6300km. (3915 miles)
Largest lake Caspian Sea (Asia) 372,000 sq. km. (143,630 sq. miles)

INDIA
Official name Bharat
Area 3,287,590 sq. km. (1,269,350 sq. miles)
Population 997,515,000
Capital New Delhi (pop. 301,000)
Largest cities Mumbai (Bombay, 12,596,000) Kolkata (Calcutta, 11,022,000) Delhi (8,419,000) Chennai (Madras, 5,422,000)
Currency Indian Rupee
Official language(s) Hindi and English (14 regional languages are also spoken)
Chief products Rice, wheat, sugar cane, jute, cotton, tea, coal, chemicals, fertilizers, vehicles
Exports Textiles, jewellery, clothing, leather goods, iron ore, tea, fish
Imports Crude oil, iron and steel, precious stones

MALDIVES
Area 298 sq. km. (115 sq. miles)
Population 200,000
Capital Malé

CHINA (PEOPLE'S REPUBLIC OF CHINA)
Official name Zhonghua Renmin Gonghe-guo
Area 9,572,383 sq. km. (3,695,918 sq. miles)
Population 1,231,571,000
Capital Beijing (Peking, pop. 11,300,000)
Largest cities Shanghai (13,580, 000) Tianjin (9,420,000) Shenyang (5,120,000) Guanzhou (Canton, 4,490,000) Harbin (4,470,000) Chengdu (4,320,000) Wuhan (4,250,000)
Currency Yuan
Official language(s) Mandarin (also Cantonese and other dialects)
Chief products Coal, iron, steel, machinery, textiles, chemicals, oil, tin, minerals, rice, tea, silkworms, pulses
Exports Livestock, textiles, ore, metals, tea, clothing
Imports Vehicles, machinery, chemicals

JAPAN
Official name Nihon
Area 377,815 sq. km. (145,875 sq. miles)
Population 126,570,000
Capital Tokyo (pop. 7,854,000)
Currency Yen
Official language(s) Japanese
Chief products Vehicles, machinery, electrical goods, iron, steel, chemicals, textiles, fish, rice
Exports steel, vehicles, electrical equipment, ships
Imports Minerals, crude oil, raw materials, food

SRI LANKA
Area 64,453 sq. km. (24,886 sq. miles)
Population 18,985,000
Capital Colombo
Chief products Graphite, minerals, precious stones

INDONESIA
Area 1,904,569 sq. km. (735,358 sq. miles)
Population 207,022,000
Capital Jakarta
Official language(s) Bahasa and Indonesian
Chief products Copra, spices, palm oil, sugar, rubber, tea, coffee, tobacco, rice, oil, timber, minerals

BHUTAN
Area 47,000 sq. km. (18,147 sq. miles)
Population 782,000
Capital Thimphu

BRUNEI
Area 5765 sq. km. (2226 sq. miles)
Population 322,000
Capital Bandar Seri Begawan

PAKISTAN
Official name Islami Jamhuriya-e-Pakistan
Area 803,943 sq. km. (310,403 sq. miles)
Population 134,790,000
Capital Islamabad
Official language(s) Urdu
Chief products Cotton, rice, wheat, sugar cane, maize, tobacco, salt, leather, wool, fertilizers, paints, carpets, paper

SINGAPORE
Area 616 sq. km. (238 sq. miles)
Population 3,952,000
Chief products Oil, refining, chemicals, ships, electrical equipment, paper, machinery, textiles

NEPAL
Area 147,181 sq. km.
(56,827 sq. miles)
Population 20,400,000
Capital Kathmandu
Chief products Cattle,
corn, rice, oil seeds, wheat

MONGOLIA
Area 1,565,000 sq. km.
(604,250 sq. miles)
Population 2,300,000
Capital Ulan Bator
Chief products Livestock,
wool, hides and skins,
minerals

NORTH KOREA
Area 120,538 sq. km.
(7929 sq. miles)
Population 23,414,000
Capital Pyongyang
Chief products Chemicals,
iron and steel, rice, corn,
machinery, wheat

SOUTH KOREA
Area 99,222 sq. km.
(38,310 sq. miles)
Population 46,858,000
Capital Seoul
Chief products Chemicals,
textiles, iron and steel,
rice, electrical equipment

BANGLADESH
Area 143,998 sq. km.
(55,598 sq. miles)
Population 127,669,000
Capital Dhaka
Chief products Jute,
paper, textiles, natural gas,
leather, rice, sugar cane

MYANMAR (BURMA)
Area 672,552 sq. km.
(261,218 sq. miles)
Population 46,500,000
Capital Yangon (Rangoon)
Chief products Silk, tin,
timber, copper, rubber

THAILAND
Area 513,115 sq. km.
(198,115 sq. miles)
Population 57,200,000
Capital Bangkok
Chief products Teak,
bamboo, fish, tin, iron ore,
natural gas, rice, rubber

LAOS
Area 236,800 sq. km.
(91,400 sq. miles)
Population 5,097,000
Capital Vientiane
Chief products Cattle,
citrus fruits, coffee, opium,
cotton, teak, rice, salt

CAMBODIA
Area 181,035 sq. km.
(69,898 sq. miles)
Population 11,757,000
Capital Phnom Penh
Chief products Cement,
paper, textiles, cattle, rice

VIETNAM
Area 328,566 sq. km.
(127,246 sq. miles)
Population 77,515,000
Capital Hanoi
Chief products Cement,
iron and steel, paper, coal,
textiles, rice

PHILIPPINES
Area 300,000 sq. km.
(115,821 sq. miles)
Population 64,600,000
Capital Manila
Chief products Fish,
pineapples, rice, metals, oil
products, mother of pearl,
mahogany, textiles

UZBEKISTAN
Area 447,400 sq. km.
(172,740 sq. miles)
Population 24,406,000
Capital Tashkent
Chief products Cotton,
vegetables, grain, paper
products, plastics

KAZAKHSTAN
Area 2,717,300 sq. km.
(1,049,155 sq. miles)
Population 14,927,000
Capital Astana
Chief products Grain,
cotton, fruit, coal, oil,
electric power

KYRGYZSTAN
Area 198,500 sq. km.
(76,640 sq. miles)
Population 4,865,000
Capital Bishkek
Chief products Grain,
vegetables, coal, oil,
cement, steel

TAJIKISTAN
Area 143,100 sq. km.
(55,250 sq. miles)
Population 6,237,000
Capital Dushanbe
Chief products Cotton,
vegetables, grain, coal, oil,
natural gas

**See page 51 for infor-
mation on other former
Soviet republics.**

BHUTAN

BRUNEI

MALDIVES

TAIWAN
Area 35,590 sq. km.
(13,890 sq. miles)
Population 22,024,000
Capital Taipei

MALAYSIA
Area 329,758 sq. km.
(127,320 sq. miles)
Population 22,710,000
Capital Kuala Lumpur
Chief products Rubber,
rice, cacao, coconuts,
minerals, palm oil, pepper

TURKMENISTAN
Area 488,100 sq. km.
(188,455 sq. miles)
Population 4,779,000
Capital Ashkhabad
Chief products Cotton,
vegetables, grain, oil,
fertilizers

The Middle East is the name given to that part of south-west Asia which lies between the Mediterranean and the Indian subcontinent. Its geographical position has led to a mix of peoples and cultures from both East and West. A series of mountain ranges runs across the north of the region from the Taurus Mountains in Turkey to the Hindu Kush, the western foothills of the Himalayas, in Afghanistan.

The climate along the Mediterranean coast is temperate but farther south the Arabian peninsula and central Iran are sparsely-populated, desert lands. The 'empty quarter' in Saudi Arabia is uninhabited except for a small number of nomadic Bedouin. Most of the population lives in the coastal regions next to the Red Sea, the Gulf and the Indian Ocean. Oil exploitation, shipping and some agriculture enable coastal communities to thrive.

Sunset over Jerusalem – city sacred to Jews, Christians and Muslims.
(top) Huts or *yurts* in the Hindu Kush region of Afghanistan, typical of those used by the Mongolian and Turkic nomads of East and Central Asia.

IRAN
Official name Jomhori-e-Islami-e-Irân
Area 1,648,000 sq. km. (636,296 sq. miles)
Population: 62,977,000
Capital: Tehran (pop. 6,759,000)
Largest cities: Mashhad (1,887,000)
Esfahan (1,266,000)
Tabriz (1,191,000)
Shiraz (1,053,000)
Karaj (941,000)
Bakhtaran (560,000)
Currency Iranian Rial
Official language(s) Farsi (Persian) (Turkish, Kurdish and Arabic are also spoken)
Chief products Oil, natural gas, iron ore, coal, zinc and lead, sugar, textiles, cement, wheat, rice, sugar beet, tobacco, fish, cotton, steel, oil seeds, wool
Exports Oil, gas, carpets, fruit, caviar, textiles, cement
Imports Livestock, minerals, chemicals, iron, steel, machinery, vehicles

ISRAEL
Official name Medinat Israel
Area 21,946 sq. km. (8473 sq. miles)
Population: 6,105,000
Capital: Jerusalem (pop. 591,000)
Largest cities: Tel Aviv-Yafo (356,000)
Haifa (252,000)
Currency New Shekel
Official language(s) Hebrew and Arabic
Chief products Citrus fruits (especially oranges), olives, rice, vegetables, tobacco, wheat, barley, corn, sesame, chemicals, clothing, finished diamonds, machinery, salts, phosphates
Exports Citrus fruits (orange), vegetables, finished diamonds, pearls, manufactured goods
Imports Rough diamonds, electrical equipment, iron and steel, chemicals, crude oil, cereals, vehicles

SAUDI ARABIA
Official name Al-Mamlaka al-Arabiya as-Sa'udiya
Area 2,400,900 sq. km. (926,745 sq. miles)
Population: 20,198,000
Capital: Riyadh (pop. 2,620,000)
Largest cities: Jiddah (Administrative capital, 1,490,000)
Mecca (770,000)
Ta'if (410,000)
Medina (400,000)
Dammam (350,000)
Hofuf (101,000)
Currency Saudi Riyal
Official language(s) Arabic
Chief products Oil, cement, fertilizers, steel, petro-chemicals, camels, citrus fruits, dates, goats, rice, vegetables, wheat
Exports Crude and refined oil
Imports Food, tobacco, metals and metal products, precision tools, precious stones, metals, ceramics, glass

TURKEY
Official name Türkiye Cumhuriyeti
Area 779,452 sq. km. (300,948 sq. miles)
Population: 64,385,000
Capital: Ankara (pop. 3,022,000)
Largest cities: Istanbul (6,407, 000)
Izmir (2,665,000)
Adana (1,430,000)
Bursa (1,031,000)
Currency Turkish Lira
Official language(s) Turkish (Kurdish is also spoken)
Chief products Iron and steel, fertilizers, machinery, vehicles, processed food and drink, paper products, textiles, barley, corn, cotton, fruit, wheat
Exports Agricultural products, textiles, tobacco, citrus fruits, figs, olives, salt, hazelnuts
Imports Machinery, iron and steel, oil, medicines, dyes, vehicles

SYRIA

Offical name Al-Jumhuriya al-Arabiya as-Souriya
Area 185,180 sq. km. (71,498 sq. miles)
Population 15,711,000
Capital Damascus
Official language(s) Arabic
Chief products Oil, natural gas, phosphates, asphalt, iron ore, tobacco, oil products, cotton

LEBANON

Official name Al-Jumhuriya al-Lubnaniya
Area 10,452 sq. km. (4036 sq. miles)
Population 4,271,000
Capital Beirut
Official language(s) Arabic (French is also spoken)
Chief products Cement, chemicals, electrical equipment, furniture, textiles, citrus fruits

JORDAN

Official name Al-Mamlaka al-Urduniya al-Hashemiyah
Area 97,740 sq. km. (37,738 sq. miles)
Population 4,740,000
Capital Amman
Official language(s) Arabic
Chief products Barley, fruit, olives, goats, lentils, sheep, vegetables, wheat, phosphates

IRAQ

Official name Al-Jumhuriya al-'Iraqiya
Area 438,317 sq. km. (169,235 sq. miles)
Population 22,797,000
Capital Baghdad
Official language(s) Arabic (Kurdish is also spoken)
Chief products Oil, dates, fruit, wheat, barley, rice, millet, cotton, tobacco, livestock, leather products

AFGHANISTAN

Official name Da Jamhuriat Afghanistan
Area 652,225 sq. km. (251,773 sq. miles)
Population 25,869,000
Capital Kabul
Official language(s) Pashtu, Dari
Chief products Cement, textiles, rugs, coal, gold, natural gas, corn, cotton, nuts, rice, sheep

Note: Turkey is defined here as part of Asia but appears partially on the map of Europe on page 25. For Cyprus's flag and details, see page 26.

KUWAIT

Official name Dawlat al-Kuwayt
Area 17,818 sq. km. (6880 sq. miles)
Population 1,924,000
Capital Kuwait
Official language(s) Arabic
Chief products Oil, natural gas, fruit, vegetables, fish (especially shrimps)

YEMEN

Official name Al-Jumhuriya al-Yemeniya
Area 477,530 sq. km. (184,345 sq. miles)
Population 17,048,000
Capital San'a
Official language(s) Arabic
Chief products Sorghum, sesame, dyes, fish, refined oil, coffee, khat, fruit, barley, cotton, dates, vegetables

OMAN

Official name Saltanat Uman
Area 271,950 sq. km. (104,970 sq. miles)
Population 2,348,000
Capital Muscat
Official language(s) Arabic (English is also spoken)
Chief products Oil, coconuts, dates, limes, livestock, sugar cane

UNITED ARAB EMIRATES

Official name Al-Imarat al-Arabiya al-Muttahida
Area 75,150 sq. km. (29,010 sq. miles)
Population 2,815,000
Capital Abu Dhabi
Official language(s) Arabic
Chief products Oil, fish (especially shrimps), dates

QATAR

Official name Dawlat Qatar
Area 11,437 sq. km. (4416 sq. miles)
Population 565,000
Capital Doha
Official language(s) Arabic (English is also spoken)
Chief products Oil and oil products

BAHRAIN

Official name Dawlat al-Bahrayn
Area 691.2 sq. km. (266.9 sq. miles)
Population 666,000
Capital Manama
Official language(s) Arabic (English is also spoken)
Chief products Oil, aluminium, boats, building materials, oil products, plastics, grains

TURKEY AND NEAR EAST

Turkey and the Near East (which includes the countries of Syria, Jordan, Lebanon and Israel) lie at the eastern end of the Mediterranean and extend south to the deserts of Saudi Arabia. People of three main religions – Islam, Judaism and Christianity – inhabit this region and all regard Jerusalem as their holy city. Religious differences and conflict over land have been the cause of many wars in the region. In 1948, the state of Israel was created in part of what had been the British Mandate of Palestine. The existence of the Jewish state is still contested by some of its Arab neighbours.

Much of Turkey and the coastal regions of Syria, Lebanon and Israel have a warm Mediterranean climate. Here the staple foods of wheat and barley are grown, as well as export crops such as tobacco, cotton, hazelnuts, citrus fruits, figs and olives. Farther east the land is hot, dry desert where agriculture is impossible without irrigation. The Dead Sea, the lowest point on the Earth, is mined for its rich salt deposits.

The 'Cotton Castle' Many tourists visit Turkey for its unspoilt beauty. These scenic chalk terraces lie inland, near Denizli. In Turkish their name is *Pamukkale* which means 'Cotton Castle'. Tourists come here to bathe in the spring water, which comes out of the ground at temperatures of up to 35 degrees Celsius.

A cotton factory in Syria
Cotton is grown extensively on the cultivated steppe lands of northeast Syria, the major agricultural region around the Euphrates and Asi rivers. This textile factory in Damascus is one of many which produces material for export. Best known is the heavy, patterned fabric *damask* which takes its name from the city.

Israel – land of the Jews
At their prayers many observant Jews wear *tephillin*, small boxes containing Hebrew scriptures that remind them to live by the Law of God.

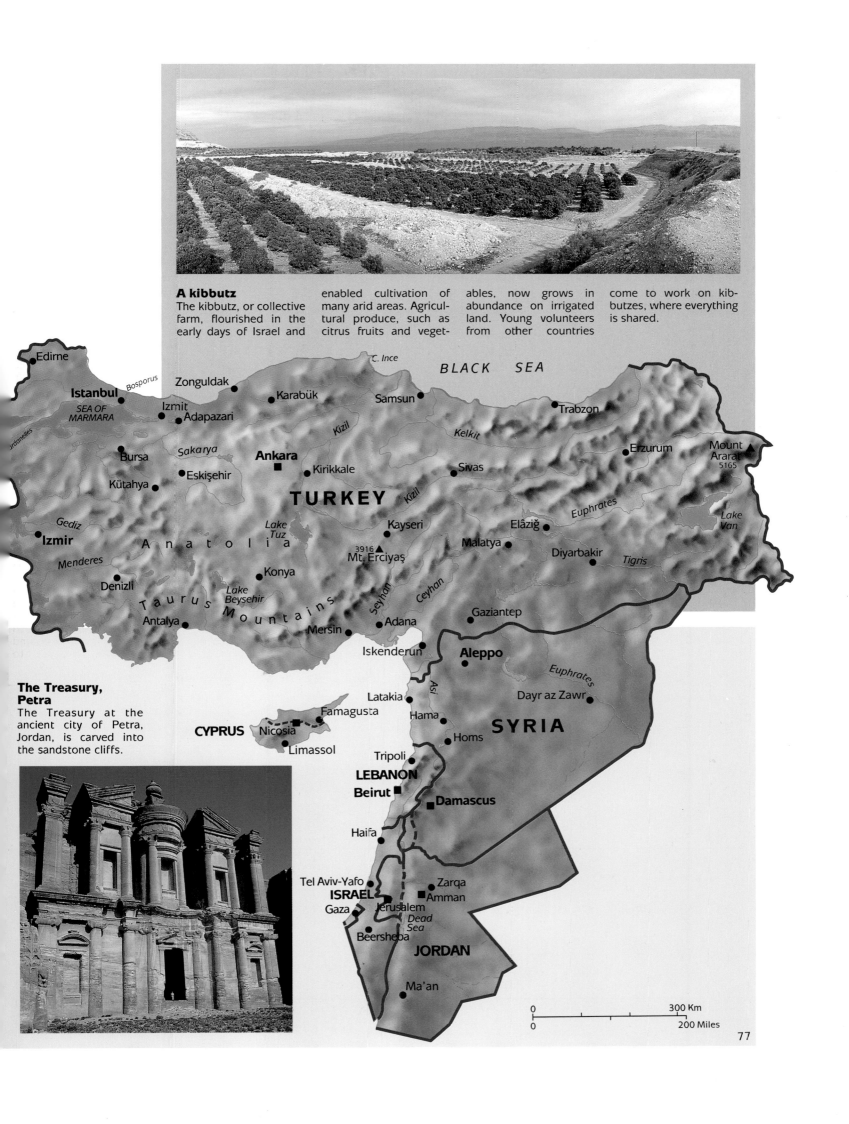

A kibbutz
The kibbutz, or collective farm, flourished in the early days of Israel and enabled cultivation of many arid areas. Agricultural produce, such as citrus fruits and vegetables, now grows in abundance on irrigated land. Young volunteers from other countries come to work on kibbutzes, where everything is shared.

The Treasury, Petra
The Treasury at the ancient city of Petra, Jordan, is carved into the sandstone cliffs.

Edirne

BLACK SEA

C. Ince

Istanbul
Bosporus
SEA OF MARMARA
Zonguldak
Izmit
Adapazari
Karabük
Samsun
Trabzon

Dardanelles

Bursa
Sakarya
Ankara
Kirikkale
Erzurum
Mount Ararat 5165

Eskişehir
Kütahya
Kizil
Sivas
Erzurum

TURKEY
Kizil
Euphrates
Lake Van

Gediz
Lake Tuz
Kayseri
Elâzığ

Izmir
A n a t o l i a
3916 Mt. Erciyaş
Malatya
Diyarbakir
Tigris

Menderes
Konya
Seyhan
Ceyhan

Denizli
Lake Beyşehir
T a u r u s M o u n t a i n s
Gaziantep

Antalya
Mersin
Adana

Iskenderun
Aleppo

Latakia
Asi
Euphrates

Famagusta
Dayr az Zawr

CYPRUS
Nicosia
Hama
SYRIA

Limassol
Homs

Tripoli

LEBANON
Beirut
Damascus

Haifa

Tel Aviv-Yafo
Zarqa
ISRAEL
Amman
Gaza
Jerusalem
Dead Sea
Beersheba
JORDAN

Ma'an

0   300 Km
0   200 Miles

ARABIAN PENINSULA

In common with all the Middle Eastern countries except Israel, the Arabian peninsula nations are mostly Islamic. The holiest of the Muslim cities, Mecca, is in Saudi Arabia. The people of this region are Arabs and they all speak a common language: Arabic.

The Arabian peninsula is a hot, dry land which is very largely desert. The only large area with enough rain to grow crops is in the highlands of Yemen. Otherwise, some farming is possible in desert 'oases', and other small areas where underground water is used to irrigate crops. The date palm is a common sight in such areas.

All the countries of the Arabian peninsula, except Yemen, have discovered large reserves of oil in recent times. Oil is pumped from underground into ships which export it to Europe, North America, Asia and Africa. The money from selling oil has made these countries very rich. Many new roads and buildings have been constructed, and some Arabs no longer ride camels as before but drive expensive cars.

Arabian desert
Parts of the desert are covered by shifting sand dunes. Some of these areas are so large they are known as 'sand seas', or *ergs* in Arabic. The *erg* of *Rub'al Khali*, or Empty Quarter, in Saudi Arabia is about the size of England and Wales put together.

A market, Yemen
At a market, or *souk*, in a town in Yemen a man weighs home-made sugared cakes before selling them. These cakes are a favourite delicacy. In many of the markets of Yemen each street has its own speciality — hats, sandals, medicinal potions, herbs, cloth and pottery are all laid out and bartered for. Shoppers fill their turbans with the day's purchases.

Oil in the Arabian peninsula

The photograph above, shows a Saudi Arabian oil refinery. Oil is the most important natural resource in the countries of the Arabian peninsula, especially those around the Persian Gulf such as Kuwait, Saudi Arabia, Qatar and the United Arab Emirates. In some parts the oil is found beneath the sea; in other areas it is beneath the desert. Once it has been extracted, most of the oil has to be transported to other countries. Oil found in southern Oman, for example, is pumped through a pipeline 450 kilometres to the north coast where it is loaded on to ships. The countries that import oil use it to make petrol, diesel, chemicals and plastics.

Saudi Arabia exports more oil than any other country in the world. Japan and the USA are its main customers. The money Saudi Arabia earns from oil is used to buy all sorts of machinery and manufactured goods, and many of these are bought from Japan and the USA. Much of the money is also spent on building things: new roads, houses, offices, airports and mosques. Saudi Arabia also buys much of its food from abroad since the people cannot grow enough of their own in the harsh climate. Saudi Arabia does not import any alcohol or any foods with pork in them. This is because the Islamic religion does not allow Muslims to eat pork or drink alcohol.

Mosque

The photograph (*left*) shows a mosque in Abu Dhabi, in the United Arab Emirates. The mosque is the Muslim place of worship. Like churches in Christian countries, mosques are often very fine buildings, some many hundreds of years old. The most important mosques have several domes and a minaret, or tower. It is from the minaret that the *muezzin*, a mosque official, will call worshippers to prayer five times a day. Most of the inhabitants of the Arabian countries are Muslims, followers of Islam. This religion teaches that there is one God, Allah, and that Mohammed was his prophet. The Koran is the sacred book of Islam.

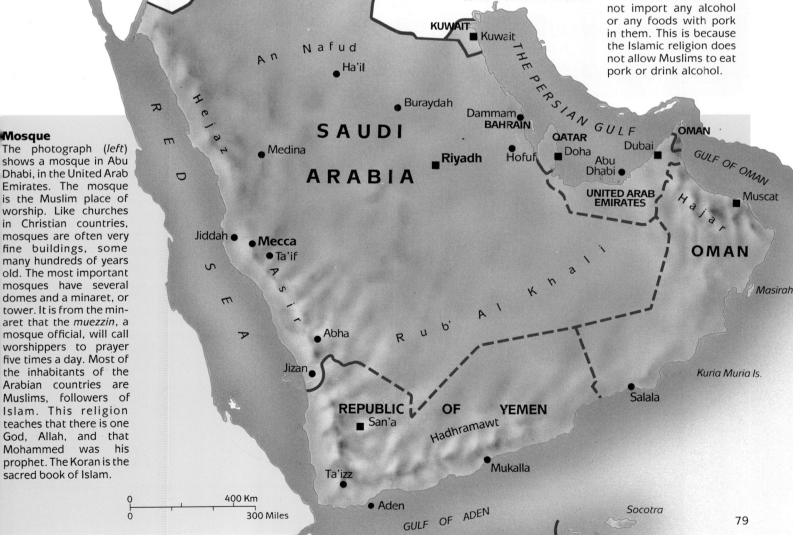

SOUTH-WEST ASIA

Between Mesopotamia and the Himalayas lie the countries of Iraq, Iran, and Afghanistan. Afghanistan is a poor country. Since 1979, civil war has ravaged the country. Many people are nomadic herders, constantly moving their animals to new grazing lands.

Iran and Iraq have become rich by exploiting their resources of oil and gas. Most of the oil is exported by tanker through the Persian Gulf, to Japan, the USA and Western Europe. Although Iran and Iraq are neighbours, religious differences and disputed territories led to war from 1980 to 1988. The Iraqis are Arabic, Sunni Muslims, whereas the Iranians are descended from Asian peoples, speak Farsi, and are Shiite Muslims. Iraq invaded Kuwait in 1990, leading to the outbreak of war in January 1991. Allied forces from the USA, Saudi Arabia, Britain, France and over twenty other nations defeated the Iraqis in February 1991.

Band-i-Amir Lake
Much of Afghanistan is desolate and bleak countryside which supports little or no vegetation. A high, inhospitable region called the Hindu Kush runs across the north-east of the country to meet the massive Hima-layan mountain range. Band-i-Amir lake (*above*) is situated in an area known as Koh-i-Baba, north-west of Kabul. It is a natural reservoir, formed by the slow build-up of mineral deposits which have trapped the water. Irri-gation ditches have been dug, and some members of the traditionally nomadic Kuchi tribe have settled on land given by the government. Others move through these remote mountain areas in search of pasture-land.

Persian carpets
The ancient tradition of carpet-making continues today in Iran. The carpets produced are better known as Persian rugs, and are prized as possessions worldwide. The rugs are worked by hand in silk or wool, using twine dyed in vivid colours and woven into intricate patterns. They are then washed and draped over rocks to dry in the sun.

The Marsh Arabs
The marshlands of southern central Iraq, around the Tigris and Euphrates rivers, are inhabited by the Marsh Arabs. The area is relatively inaccessible and as a result the Marsh Arabs' traditional way of life has remained almost untouched by outside influences. Many people still live in reed houses built on piles of rushes in up to two metres of water. Transport is by elegant canoes.

Persepolis, southern Iran

The ruins of the great palace of Persepolis as they stand today in southern Iran. Building work was started on the palace in 520BC under the order of Darius the First, ruler of the Persian Empire which covered much of modern Iran, Iraq, Afghanistan and the Near East. Darius and his court used Persepolis only once a year, at New Year, when tribute was brought to him by the various peoples of his vast empire. Some of these tribute-bearers are depicted on the great staircase in the foreground of this picture.

Praying towards Mecca

Every aspect of a Muslim's life is guided by the principles of Islam. Many of the rights and duties by which a Muslim should live are written in the Koran, the holy book of Islam that records the word of God as told to the prophet Muhammad. Among these duties are that all Muslim men and women should profess belief in the one God and pray to him five times each day, facing in the direction of Mecca. At the mosque, one of the walls has a special niche which shows this direction.

SOUTH ASIA

The region of South Asia is often called the Indian sub-continent. In the north, the high, snow-clad peaks and valleys of the Himalayas are sparsely populated. Farther south, overcrowded cities, such as Kolkata (Calcutta) and Mumbai (Bombay) are home to millions of people, many of whom live on the streets or in shanty towns.

Both India and Bangladesh have huge, and growing populations – over 800 million people live in India alone. In the past people have settled here from all over Asia, and more than 200 languages are still spoken across the region. Hinduism and Buddhism, two of the world's major religions, started in this area. Today, Pakistan and Bangladesh are mainly Muslim states and India is predominantly Hindu.

Rice, wheat and cotton are important crops and both India and Pakistan are major textile exporters. However, much agriculture is still subsistence farming, and relies on the annual monsoon rains which fall between June and October.

Que

PA

Baluchistan

Central Makran Ra

Karach

An Indian spice seller

This man is sitting at his spice stall in an Indian bazaar. Spices are very important in Indian food – one of the most popular dishes is highly-spiced curry. Some of the most common spices are pepper, ginger, mustard and cinnamon.

For centuries India has had a flourishing spice trade with countries in the West. Before refrigeration was invented, spices were used to disguise the taste and smell of food that was not fresh.

Rice-growing in Pakistan

Rice is the main crop grown in the Punjab region of Pakistan. The rice-fields are flooded with water taken from the River Indus. Oxen are still used for the heavy labour.

The River Ganges at Varanasi

These Hindus are bathing in the River Ganges because the waters are believed to be holy. Every year millions of pilgrims come to the sacred Indian city of Varanasi to wash away their sins.

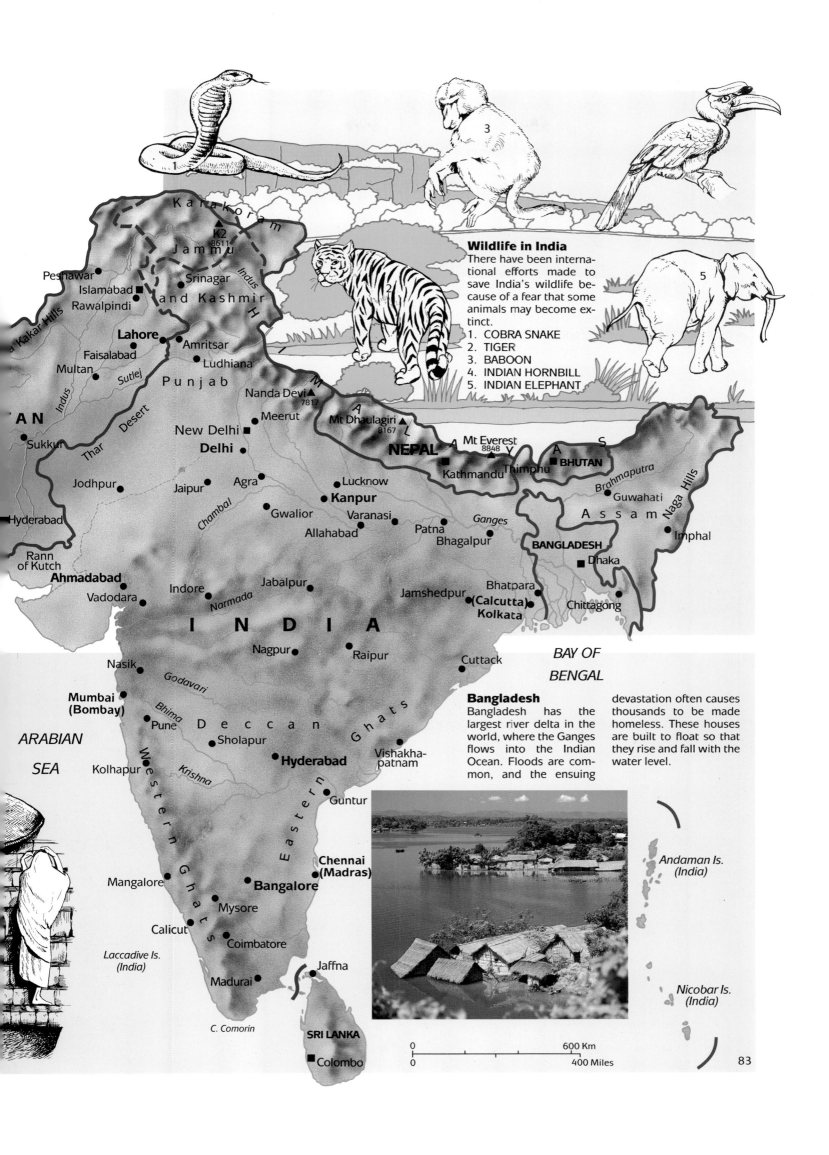

Wildlife in India

There have been international efforts made to save India's wildlife because of a fear that some animals may become extinct.
1. COBRA SNAKE
2. TIGER
3. BABOON
4. INDIAN HORNBILL
5. INDIAN ELEPHANT

Karakoram

K2
8611

Jammu

Srinagar

Indus

and Kashmir

Peshawar

Islamabad

Rawalpindi

Kakar Hills

Lahore

Amritsar

Faisalabad

Ludhiana

Multan

Sutlej

Punjab

Indus

Desert

Nanda Devi
7817

Meerut

Mt Dhaulagiri
8167

Mt Everest
8848

NEPAL

Thimphu

BHUTAN

New Delhi

Delhi

Kathmandu

Brahmaputra

Thar

Jodhpur

Jaipur

Agra

Lucknow

Guwahati

Naga Hills

AN

Sukkur

Kanpur

Assam

Hyderabad

Gwalior

Varanasi

Ganges

Allahabad

Patna

Bhagalpur

Imphal

Chambal

Rann
of Kutch

Ahmadabad

BANGLADESH

Dhaka

Vadodara

Indore

Jabalpur

Narmada

Jamshedpur

Bhatpara

(Calcutta)

Kolkata

Chittagong

I N D I A

Nagpur

Raipur

Nasik

Cuttack

BAY OF
BENGAL

Godavari

Mumbai
(Bombay)

Bhima

Pune

D e c c a n

Sholapur

Eastern Ghats

ARABIAN

SEA

Western Ghats

Kolhapur

Krishna

Hyderabad

Vishakha-
patnam

Bangladesh

Bangladesh has the largest river delta in the world, where the Ganges flows into the Indian Ocean. Floods are common, and the ensuing devastation often causes thousands to be made homeless. These houses are built to float so that they rise and fall with the water level.

Guntur

Mangalore

Chennai
(Madras)

Bangalore

Andaman Is.
(India)

Mysore

Calicut

Coimbatore

Laccadive Is.
(India)

Jaffna

Madurai

Nicobar Is.
(India)

C. Comorin

SRI LANKA

Colombo

0		600 Km
0		400 Miles

SOUTH-EAST ASIA

The region known as south-east Asia includes more than 20,000 islands, mostly in Indonesia and the Philippines. Indonesia is the largest archipelago in the world, spanning 5120 kilometres – nearly the width of the USA.

The staple crop of the area is rice. Thailand, in particular, is known as the 'rice-bowl of Asia'. Other crops include coffee, rubber, sugar cane and coconuts. Most of the countries of this region have economies based on agriculture, and are relatively undeveloped. In contrast, Singapore is an international port and commercial centre, and Brunei, a tiny kingdom on the north coast of Borneo, is rich from oil. Indonesia, too, exports oil and has a lucrative and thriving tourist industry.

Mining in south-east Asia

Tin is mined throughout Malaysia and is a major source of income for the country.

Mining techniques are often basic, but modern technology is being introduced. From ports such as Port Kelang vast quantities of tin and Malaysia's other major commodity, rubber, are exported.

Teak logging

In Thailand's northern forests, domesticated elephants move felled teak trees to the saw mills. The elephants are used for their massive strength and mobility on ground which is unsuitable for heavy machinery.

MYANMAR
(BURMA)

Mandalay

Irrawaddy

Hanoi

Luang Prabang

Chiang Mai

Vientiane

L A O S

Rangoon

Moulmein

THAILAND

Mekong

Bangkok

Tonle Sap

Andaman Is.
(India)

CAMBODIA

Phnom Penh

Gulf
of
Thailand

Kota Baharu

M A

Peninsular
Malaysia

Bunga
Is.

Medan

Kuala
Lumpur

Anamb

L. Toba

Nias

Sumatra

SINGAPORE

Padang

Bangk

Palembang

Belitu

Teluk
Betung

Enggano

Jakarta

Krakatau

Bandung

J

0   500 Km
0   400 Miles

Wildlife

Two exotic examples of the wildlife of the region are shown here.
1. PROBOSCIS MONKEY
2. MALAYAN TAPIR

Balinese dancers

These two young Balinese dancers are performing the graceful *legong* dance wearing flower headpieces and dazzling costumes. Such dances were originally performed to please the gods during festivals, when temples throughout the island were decorated with flowers and food offerings for them. Though they still play an important part in village life, many of the traditional rituals are now more often performed for the tourists who come to enjoy this tropical paradise.

The Shwesandaw Pagoda

The Shwesandaw Pagoda, the most highly revered religious building in Myanmar (Burma), is situated on the eastern bank of the River Irrawaddy, eight kilometres south of Pyè.

Buddhism is the main religion in this region. Every village has at least one monastery, and orange-clad monks are a common sight.

Batan Is.

Babuyan Is.

Luzon

Quezon City

Manila

Mindoro

PHILIPPINES

Samar

Panay

Cebu

Negros

Palawan

SULU SEA

Mindanao

Davao

Sulu Arch.

Jang

TNAM

Minh City

SOUTH CHINA SEA

Bandar Seri Begawan
BRUNEI

Sabah

▲ Kinabalu
4101

YSIA

Sarawak

Kuching   *Borneo*

Kapuas   Mahakam

Kalimantan

Barito

Banjarmasin

JAVA SEA

INDONESIA

Ujung Pandang

Semarang

Yogyakarta   *Madura*

Malang   **Surabaya**

Bali

Lombok

Sumba

Sumbawa

Lesser Sunda Islands

Flores

Timor

FLORES SEA

Wetar

Alor

CELEBES SEA

Manado

Halmahera

Sula Is.

Sulawesi (Celebes)

Buru

Moluccas

Ceram

Butung

BANDA SEA

Tanimbar Islands

Biak

Aru Is.

Maloke Range
▲ Puncak Jaya
5029

West Papua

Jayapura

CHINA AND KOREA

This region covers a vast area of eastern Asia, running from the barren hills and plains of the Gobi, a vast desert in Mongolia, south to the Tibetan Plateau and east to the fertile plains and river valleys of China.

China itself is roughly the same size as the USA, yet its population is more than four times as big, and it is one of the poorest countries in the world. Much of the population is concentrated in the south-east of the country, where rice and tea are cultivated, and silk is produced.

There are mineral reserves of coal, iron ore, oil and gas, mainly in the west. Industry has developed in and around such cities as Beijing (Peking) and in Shanghai, where textiles and electrical goods are manufactured for export.

A Chinese canal scene
On the Great Plain in eastern China there are numerous canals which link up with some of the country's rivers. The canals bring water to dry districts and are used as transport routes. In this picture, two men are steering their barge with a cargo of hay through a town, the canal banks crowded with ramshackle houses.

The Potala Palace in Tibet
The Potala Palace stands on a high mount overlooking the city of Lhasa in the Himalayan mountains. It was once the residence of the Dalai Lama who is Tibet's spiritual leader, but in 1959 he was forced to leave the country by the Chinese Communists. Lhasa is a holy city for Tibetan Buddhists who worship the statue of Buddha in the temple of the Potala Palace.

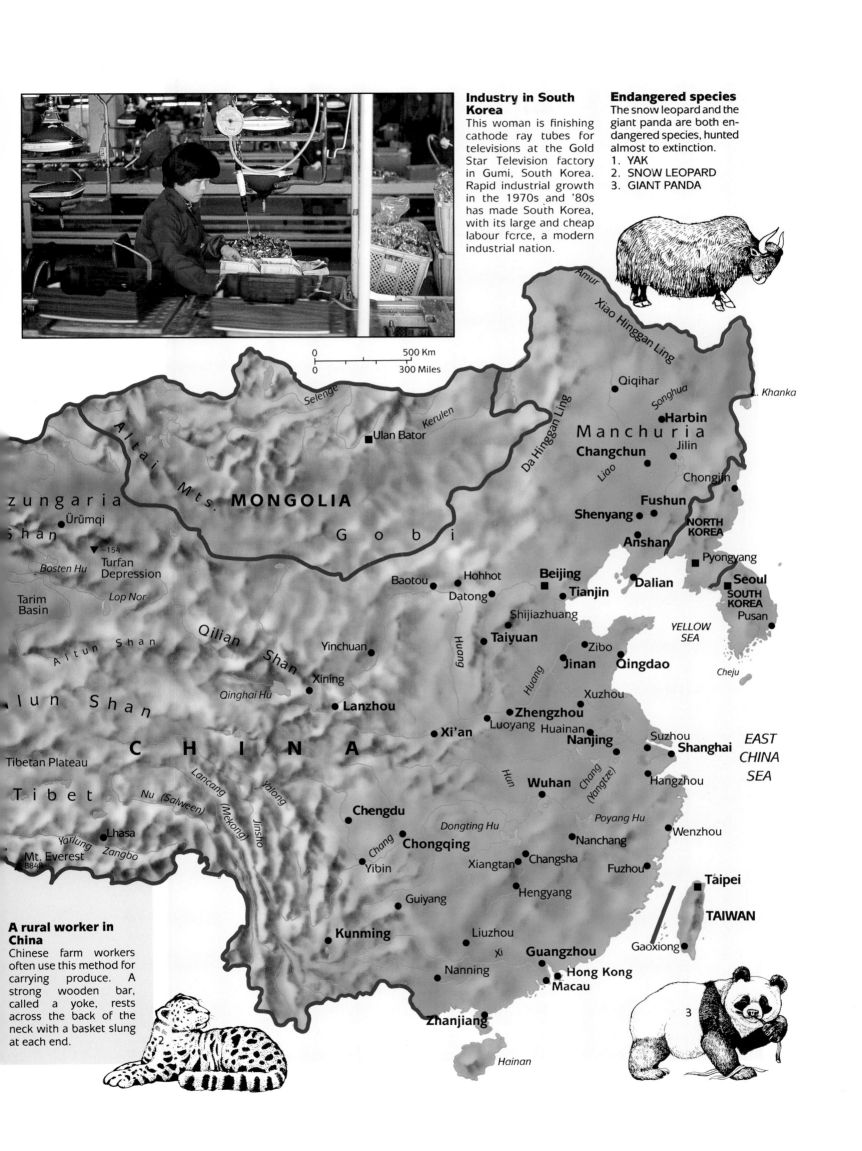

Industry in South Korea

This woman is finishing cathode ray tubes for televisions at the Gold Star Television factory in Gumi, South Korea. Rapid industrial growth in the 1970s and '80s has made South Korea, with its large and cheap labour force, a modern industrial nation.

Endangered species

The snow leopard and the giant panda are both endangered species, hunted almost to extinction.
1. YAK
2. SNOW LEOPARD
3. GIANT PANDA

A rural worker in China

Chinese farm workers often use this method for carrying produce. A strong wooden bar, called a yoke, rests across the back of the neck with a basket slung at each end.

0   500 Km
0   300 Miles

Altai Mts.

zungaria
Shan
Ürümqi
Bosten Hu
Turfan Depression
−154
Lop Nor
Tarim Basin
Altun Shan
lun Shan
Qilian Shan
Qinghai Hu
Xining
Lanzhou

MONGOLIA

Gobi

Selenge
Kerulen
Ulan Bator

Xiao Hinggan Ling
Amur
Da Hinggan Ling
Songhua
Qiqihar
L. Khanka

Manchuria
Harbin
Changchun
Jilin
Chongjin
Fushun
Shenyang
Anshan
NORTH KOREA
Pyongyang

Baotou
Hohhot
Datong
Beijing
Tianjin
Dalian
Seoul
SOUTH KOREA
Pusan

Shijiazhuang
Taiyuan
Zibo
Jinan
Qingdao
YELLOW SEA
Cheju

Huang
Xuzhou
Yinchuan

Tibetan Plateau
Tibet
Mt. Everest
8848
Lhasa
Yarlung Zangbo
Nu (Salween)
Lancang (Mekong)
Yalong
Jinsho
Chang
Yibin

CHINA

Xi'an
Zhengzhou
Luoyang
Huainan
Nanjing
Suzhou
Shanghai
Hangzhou

Hun
Wuhan
Chang (Yangtze)

EAST CHINA SEA

Chengdu
Dongting Hu
Poyang Hu
Chongqing
Nanchang
Wenzhou
Xiangtan
Changsha
Fuzhou
Hengyang

Guiyang
Taipei
TAIWAN

Kunming
Liuzhou
Guangzhou
Xi
Nanning
Hong Kong
Macau
Gaoxiong

Zhanjiang
Hainan

3

JAPAN

Japan forms an archipelago in the Pacific comprising four main islands: Honshu, Hokkaido, Shikoku and Kyushu, and over 3000 smaller, mostly uninhabited ones. This region is an earthquake zone and has over 50 active volcanoes. About seventy per cent of the country is mountainous and covered with forests, and most people live on the coastal plains.

The climate is subtropical in the south and colder in the north. On Hokkaido there is snow for up to four months in the winter. The warm-water Kuroshio Current brings a rainy season to the south in June and early July.

Japan is one of the world's most successful industrial nations, producing cars, motorcycles, electrical goods and over one third of the world's ships. All the raw materials to make these – such as iron ore, oil and coal – have to be imported as Japan has almost no natural resources. Japan is also one of the major fishing nations, catching large amounts of tuna, squid and octopus for its home market.

A Japanese garden
The Japanese are famous for their garden design. In the past many European gardens were modelled on Japanese styles with pagodas, teahouses, bridges and stone lanterns arranged around a pool or stream. Over the centuries growing trees has also developed into a sophisticated art in Japan – especially miniature trees like the bonsai, which are grown in pots.

Karatsu Kunchi festival
The colourful Karatsu Kunchi festival takes place between 2 and 4 November. It is the autumn festival of the Karatsu Shrine. Fourteen impressive decorated floats are drawn through Karatsu city. Among other things, the floats depict a red lion, a turtle, Samurai helmets and a red sea bream, shown here in the photograph.

The Japanese at work

In large Japanese corporations today it is quite common for workers to participate in morning exercise routines on the factory floor. Many Japanese employees also wear a company uniform and take pride in their teamwork.

The people of Japan have become known worldwide as hard-working and efficient, and are world leaders in the electronics field. Robots and advanced computers are used to produce the latest in household technology, such as microwave ovens, camcorders, video cassette recorders and stereos.

The tea ceremony

Although Japan is a modern westernized society, old traditions are carefully preserved. The tea ceremony is an ancient ritual that many Japanese still continue to learn and practise. The bitter, green tea is served in delicate china and drunk slowly and reverently.

Harvesting rice

Farmers in this rice-field are gathering the rice into bundles to dry before threshing. Farming equipment is specially designed for Japanese farms, which are very small. Only fifteen per cent of the land in Japan is suitable for cultivation.

La Perouse Strait

Rebun
C. Soya
Rishiri
Wakkanai

0
300 Km
0
200 Miles

Asahikawa

Hokkaido

Ishikari
Sapporo
Kushiro

Okushiri

C. Erimo

Hakodate

Tsugaru Str.
C. Shiriya

Aomori

Akita

SEA OF

JAPAN

Sendai

JAPAN

Sado

Niigata

C. Suzu

Koriyama

Shinano

Iwaki

Nagano
Utsunomiya

Kanazawa
Toyama
Maebashi

Tone

Oki Is.

Honshu
Tokyo
Kawasaki
Yokohama
Chiba

Gifu
Mt. Fuji
3776
Yokosuka

L. Biwa

Kyoto
Nagoya
Shizuoka

Tsu
Shima

Okayama
Himeji
Toyohashi

Kobe
Hamamatsu

Hiroshima
Osaka
Sakai

Shimonoseki
Kure
Takamatsu
Wakayama

Kitakyushu
Matsuyama
Tokushima

Fukuoka
Kochi
C. Shio

Sasebo
Shikoku

Nagasaki
Oita
Kumamoto

Kyushu

Kagoshima

Osumi Is.
Tanega

Yaku

Amami

Tokuno
Ryukyu Islands

Okinawa

AFRICA

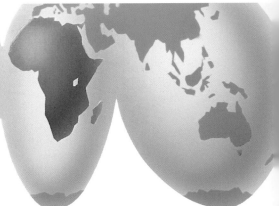

Africa is the second largest continent, stretching south from the Mediterranean Sea and lying between the Atlantic and the Indian Oceans. It is a land of infinite contrast. Much of northern Africa is covered by the Sahara, the biggest and hottest desert in the world, larger in size than the whole of Australia. In western and central regions, large areas of the coast are covered by dense tropical rainforests.

The Great Rift Valley runs from the Red Sea south to Malawi. East of the Rift are the mountain ranges of Ethiopia, Kenya and Tanzania, including the highest mountain peak in Africa, Kilimanjaro at 5895 metres. High plateaus in eastern and southern Africa are covered by rolling grasslands, known as savanna, home to much of Africa's abundant wildlife.

Open grassland, or *veldt*, in Drakensberg, on the border between South Africa and Lesotho.

Africa
Highest point Kilimanjaro (Tanzania) 5895m. (19,340ft.) above sea level
Lowest point Lake Assal (Djibouti) 155m. (509ft.) below sea level
Longest river Nil (Eygpt) 6671km. (414 miles)
Largest lake Victori (Kenya/Uganda/ Tanzania) 69,484 sq km. (26,828 sq. miles)

MOROCCO
Area 458,775 sq. km. (177,070 sq. miles)
Population 28,238,000
Capital Rabat
Chief products Clay, lead, marble, cement, food, soap, leather, textiles, almonds

GHANA
Area 238,537 sq. km. (92,100 sq. miles)
Population 18,785,000
Capital Accra
Chief products Textiles, bauxite, diamonds, gold, manganese, cacao, coffee

LIBYA
Area 1,775,500 sq. km. (685,524 sq. miles)
Population 5,419,000
Capital Tripoli
Chief products Oil, citrus fruits, dates, barley, olives, livestock, wheat

ALGERIA
Area 2,381,741 sq. km. (919,595 sq. miles)
Population 29,950,000
Capital Algiers
Chief products Iron ore, oil, phosphates, fruit, grain, vegetables, wine

NIGERIA
Area 923,768 sq. km. (356,669 sq. miles)
Population 123,897,000
Capital Abuja
Chief products Oil, tin, limestone, rubber, rice, chemicals, beans, cacao

EGYPT
Area 997,738 sq. km. (385,229 sq. miles)
Population 62,655,000
Capital Cairo
Chief products Iron ore, oil, manganese, salt, fish, cement, fertilizers, steel

ETHIOPIA
Area 1,128,219 sq. km. (435,606 sq. miles)
Population 62,782,000
Capital Addis Ababa
Chief products Barley, beans, coffee, cotton, hides and skins, livestock, timber

DEM. REP. CONGO
Area 2,344,885 sq. km. (905,365 sq. miles)
Population 49,776,000
Capital Kinshasa
Chief products Cement, industrial diamonds, oil, coffee, cottoh, copper, gold

CÔTE D'IVOIRE
Area 322,462 sq. km. (124,503 sq. miles)
Population 15,545,000
Capital Yamoussoukro
Chief products Textiles, fruit, electrical equipment, ships, textiles, timber

CAMEROON
Area 475,442 sq. km. (183,569 sq. miles)
Population 14,691,000
Capital Yaoundé
Chief products Aluminium, oil, timber, natural rubber, bananas, cassava, cacao

SUDAN
Area 2,505,813 sq. km. (967,500 sq. miles)
Population 28,993,000
Capital Khartoum
Chief products Cotton, corn, dates, hides, skins, melons, peanuts, salt

KENYA
Area 580,367 sq. km. (224,081 sq. miles)
Population 29,410,000
Capital Nairobi
Chief products Coffee, corn, tea, sisal, sugar cane, cement, chemicals

UGANDA
Area 231,860 sq. km. (91,343 sq. miles)
Population 21,479,000
Capital Kampala
Chief products Copper, bananas, coffee, cotton, sweet potatoes, tea

Name	Area sq. km. (sq. miles)	Population	Capital
Angola	1,246,700 (481,354)	12,357,000	Luanda
Benin	112,622 (43,484)	6,114,000	Porto Novo
Botswana	582,000 (224,711)	1,588,000	Gaborone
Burkina Faso	274,200 (105,870)	10,996,000	Ouagadougou
Burundi	27,834 (10,747)	6,678,000	Bujumbura
Cape Verde	4033 (1557)	428,000	Praia
Central African Republic	622,984 (240,535)	3,540,000	Bangui
Chad	1,284,000 (495,800)	7,486,000	Ndjamena
Comoros	1862 (719)	544,000	Moroni
Djibouti	23,200 (8958)	648,000	Djibouti
Equatorial Guinea	28,051 (10,830)	443,000	Malabo
Eritrea	94,000 (36,293)	3,991,000	Asmara
Gabon	267,667 (103,347)	1,208,000	Libreville
The Gambia	11,295 (4361)	1,251,000	Banjul
Guinea	245,857 (94,926)	7,251,000	Conakry
Guinea-Bissau	36,125 (13,948)	1,185,000	Bissau
Lesotho	30,355 (11,720)	2,105,000	Maseru
Liberia	97,754 (37,743)	3,044,000	Monrovia
Madagascar	587,041 (226,658)	15,051,000	Antananarivo
Malawi	94,080 (36,315)	10,788,000	Lilongwe
Mali	1,240,190 (478,770)	10,584,000	Bamako
Mauritania	1,030,700 (397,950)	2,958,000	Nouakchott
Mauritius	2040 (788)	1,174,000	Port Louis
Namibia	824,292 (318,261)	1,701,000	Windhoek
Niger	1,267,000 (489,191)	10,496,000	Niamey
Republic of Congo	342,000 (132,047)	2,859,000	Brazzaville
Réunion (Fr.)	2512 (968.5)	707,000	Saint-Denis
Rwanda	26,338 (10,169)	8,310,000	Kigali
São Tomé and Principe	964 (372)	145,000	São Tomé
Senegal	196,722 (75,955)	9,285,000	Dakar
Seychelles	454 (175)	80,000	Victoria
Sierra Leone	71,740 (27,699)	4,949,000	Freetown
Somalia	637,657 (246,201)	9,388,000	Mogadishu
Swaziland	17,363 (6704)	1,019,000	Mbabane
Togo	56,785 (21,925)	4,567,000	Lomé
Tunisia	163,610 (63,170)	9,457,000	Tunis

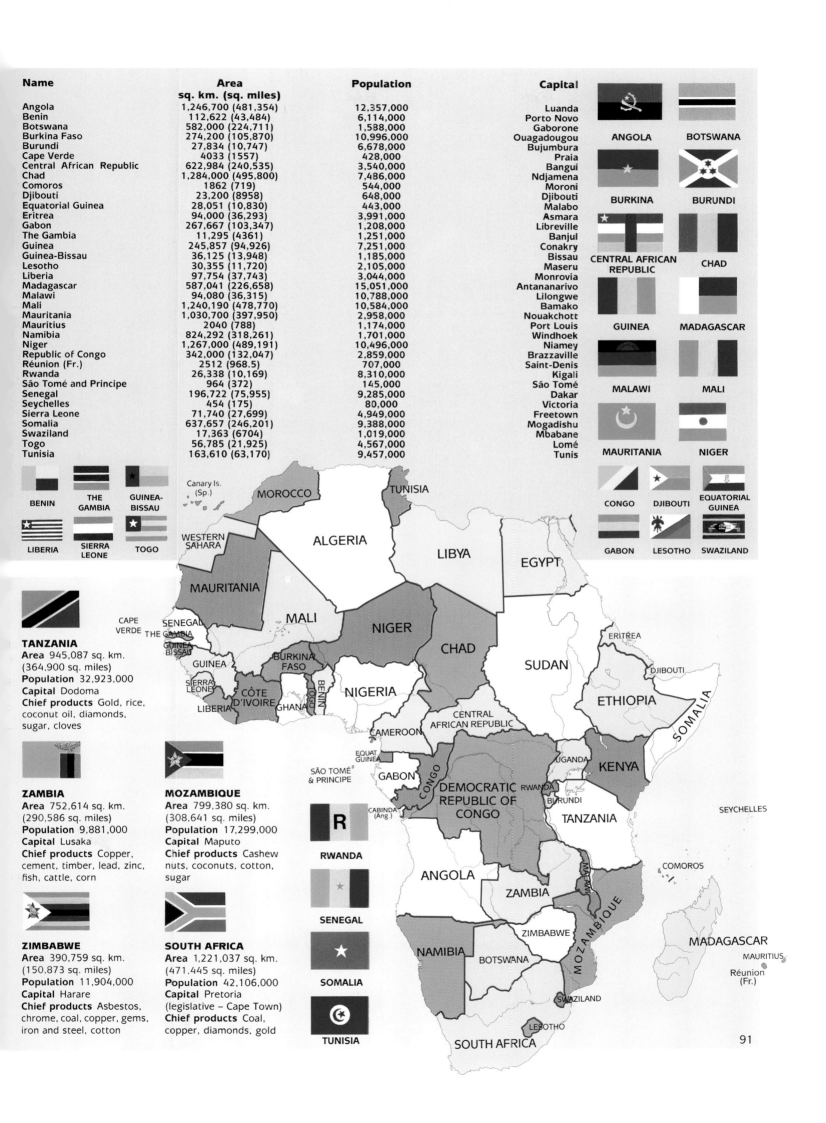

ANGOLA

BOTSWANA

BURKINA

BURUNDI

CENTRAL AFRICAN REPUBLIC

CHAD

GUINEA

MADAGASCAR

MALAWI

MALI

MAURITANIA

NIGER

CONGO

DJIBOUTI

EQUATORIAL GUINEA

GABON

LESOTHO

SWAZILAND

BENIN

THE GAMBIA

GUINEA-BISSAU

LIBERIA

SIERRA LEONE

TOGO

TANZANIA
Area 945,087 sq. km. (364,900 sq. miles)
Population 32,923,000
Capital Dodoma
Chief products Gold, rice, coconut oil, diamonds, sugar, cloves

ZAMBIA
Area 752,614 sq. km. (290,586 sq. miles)
Population 9,881,000
Capital Lusaka
Chief products Copper, cement, timber, lead, zinc, fish, cattle, corn

MOZAMBIQUE
Area 799,380 sq. km. (308,641 sq. miles)
Population 17,299,000
Capital Maputo
Chief products Cashew nuts, coconuts, cotton, sugar

RWANDA

SENEGAL

SOMALIA

TUNISIA

ZIMBABWE
Area 390,759 sq. km. (150,873 sq. miles)
Population 11,904,000
Capital Harare
Chief products Asbestos, chrome, coal, copper, gems, iron and steel, cotton

SOUTH AFRICA
Area 1,221,037 sq. km. (471,445 sq. miles)
Population 42,106,000
Capital Pretoria (legislative – Cape Town)
Chief products Coal, copper, diamonds, gold

NORTHERN AFRICA

North Africa is dominated by the Sahara, which stretches 4800 kilometres from the Atlantic coast in Mauritania across to the Red Sea in Sudan. It is the largest desert in the world; moreover, drought and destructive farming methods are causing it to expand southwards at the rate of about ten kilometres a year. The climate along the Mediterranean coast enables crops such as dates and fruit to be grown, particularly in the foothills of the Atlas Mountains in the northwest. Huge irrigation systems are being developed by oil-rich Libya to pump water from deep beneath the desert to the fertile coastal areas 900 kilometres away. However, farther south in Sudan and the highlands of Ethiopia, crop failures and drought have caused widespread famine.

Traditionally, the Arab world has had a great influence on northern Africa, particularly in Egypt. The people of the region are mostly Muslim, and Arabic is widely spoken.

The River Nile

Much of Egypt is desert land which cannot support vegetation. The fertile regions on either side of the River Nile and in the Nile delta form the major agricultural areas.

The River Nile is controlled by the Aswan Dam, completed in 1965, and now flows steadily all year, providing a constant supply of water for irrigation. Before the dam was built, the Nile regularly flooded its banks, washing nutrient-rich mud on to the land.

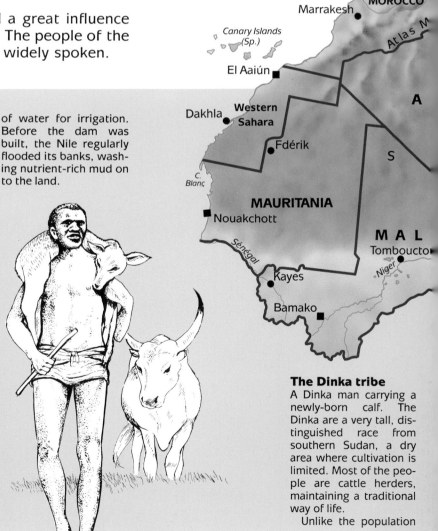

The Dinka tribe

A Dinka man carrying a newly-born calf. The Dinka are a very tall, distinguished race from southern Sudan, a dry area where cultivation is limited. Most of the people are cattle herders, maintaining a traditional way of life.

Unlike the population

Ethiopia's famine

Ethiopia has been hit by severe drought for many years in succession. Lack of rain has meant that crops and livestock have perished, leaving many millions of people starving. There was a severe drought in 1973, but it was little publicized. In 1974 a Communist revolution overthrew Haile Selassie, who was emperor at that time, and since then drought and warfare have together caused widespread suffering. After 31 years of fierce fighting, the northern province of Eritrea won independence from Addis Ababa's rule in 1993. Although just a bit larger than Portugal, nine ethnic groups, about evenly split between Muslim and Christian, live there, speaking seven native languages.

The devastating famine of 1985 was brought to the attention of the whole world, particularly by the pop music charity, Band Aid,

A Moroccan *souk*

All major towns in Morocco feature a bazaar, or *souk*, selling local and imported goods in noisy and colourful surroundings. Exotic items are sold including brassware, jewellery, spices and perfumes and fresh local produce is available too. Other activities include leather tanning and wool dying.

which organized the Live Aid international music festival. The revenue from this enabled international aid agencies such as the Red Cross and OXFAM to provide medical supplies, food and shelter to many of the worst affected areas.

of the north, the people of southern Sudan, such as the Dinka and the Nuer, are not Muslim and do not speak Arabic. Conflict arising from these differences led to civil war in the 1980s and '90s. The spread of Islam and Arabic from the north continues to be a threat to the people of the south.

WESTERN, CENTRAL AND EASTERN AFRICA

In western Africa the Gulf of Guinea is bordered by many relatively small countries. Agriculture is important, and crops such as cocoa, palm oil and groundnuts, as well as hardwood trees are grown for export. Nigeria, the most populous country in Africa, has benefited from the discovery of large oil reserves in the late 1950s. Oil revenues have been used to finance new industries such as petro-chemical production, steel-making and vehicle manufacture.

Dense tropical rainforests lie across central Africa, through which flows the River Congo. Like much of Africa, the countries of this region are made up of peoples of many ethnic groups – more than 250 languages are spoken in the Democratic Republic of Congo. To the east of the Great Rift Valley the flat grasslands of Tanzania and Kenya are sparsely populated by the Masai and other cattle herders. The climate in this region is particularly suited to growing coffee and tea, which are major exports.

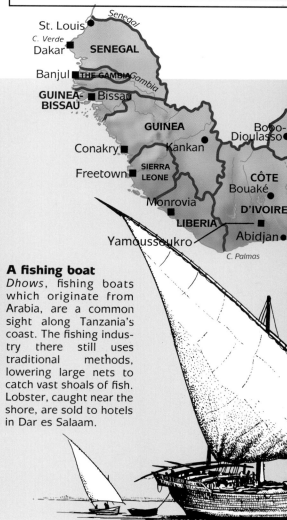

Lagos, Nigeria

Nigeria has a population of almost 108 million, the largest in Africa, made up of 250 different ethnic groups including the Hausa, Yoruba and Ibo peoples. Lagos, the main city, is a thriving port on the south-west coast. The heart of the city, Lagos island, contains the administrative sector and is linked to the mainland and other islands by road bridges.

Huge oil reserves, discovered in the 1950s, have enabled Nigeria to build roads and ports and set up new industries. Despite this industrial development, Nigeria is still unable to produce enough food for its rapidly increasing population.

A fishing boat

Dhows, fishing boats which originate from Arabia, are a common sight along Tanzania's coast. The fishing industry there still uses traditional methods, lowering large nets to catch vast shoals of fish. Lobster, caught near the shore, are sold to hotels in Dar es Salaam.

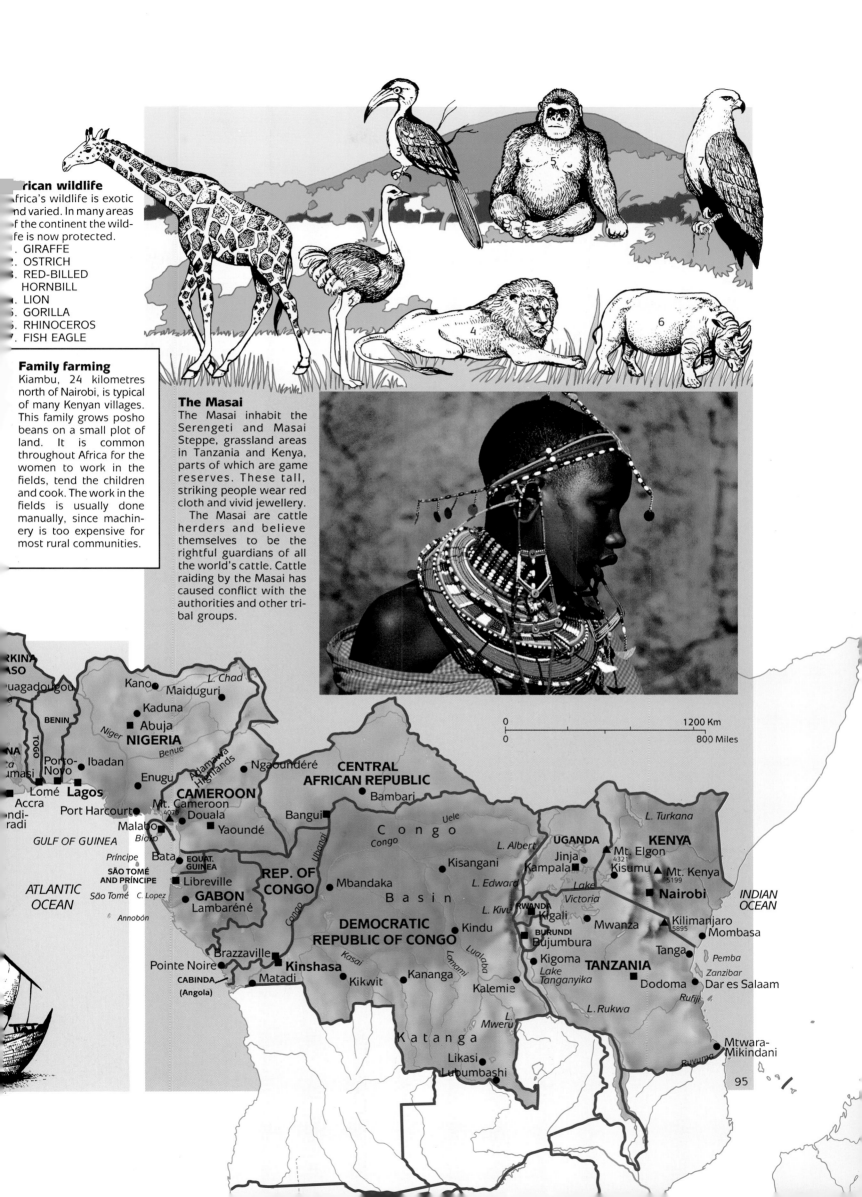

African wildlife

Africa's wildlife is exotic and varied. In many areas of the continent the wildlife is now protected.

1. GIRAFFE
2. OSTRICH
3. RED-BILLED HORNBILL
4. LION
5. GORILLA
6. RHINOCEROS
7. FISH EAGLE

Family farming

Kiambu, 24 kilometres north of Nairobi, is typical of many Kenyan villages. This family grows posho beans on a small plot of land. It is common throughout Africa for the women to work in the fields, tend the children and cook. The work in the fields is usually done manually, since machinery is too expensive for most rural communities.

The Masai

The Masai inhabit the Serengeti and Masai Steppe, grassland areas in Tanzania and Kenya, parts of which are game reserves. These tall, striking people wear red cloth and vivid jewellery.

The Masai are cattle herders and believe themselves to be the rightful guardians of all the world's cattle. Cattle raiding by the Masai has caused conflict with the authorities and other tribal groups.

SOUTHERN AFRICA

A ngola, Zambia, Mozambique and the countries farther south are all part of southern Africa. The landscape varies from the hot, dry areas of the Namib and Kalahari deserts, to the vast, open grasslands of the *veld* in South Africa and the lush low-lying plains of Mozambique.

The economies of most of the southern African countries rely heavily on the export of minerals. The region contains great concentrations of valuable mineral resources. Botswana, South Africa and Zimbabwe have some of the world's richest diamond deposits as well as huge coal reserves.

On 10 May 1994, Nelson Mandela, who had spent 26 years in prison for his political activities, was elected the first black president of South Africa. The elections were the first in which blacks were allowed to vote, and marked the end of apartheid, a system which had kept the black majority separate from and unequal to the white minority. The new government headed by Mandela included blacks, whites, Asians, and Coloureds (people of mixed origin).

Kokerboom Forest, Namibia
The Kokerboom tree is also known as the quiver tree, because the Bushmen used to make pincushion-type quivers for their arrows from its fibrous core. The trees thrive in the arid land of central Namibia because they store water and can resist drought for years.

Agriculture in Zambia
In order to provide food for Africa's ever-growing population, agriculture must be developed. One option is to improve farming techniques in the villages. Alternatively, large-scale projects can be adopted, such as the Mpongwe scheme in Zambia which produces soya beans.

San people of the Kalahari
San people (formerly called Bushmen) make jewellery from tiny fragments of ostrich shells.

Mineral resources in southern Africa

Rich mineral deposits exist throughout southern and south-western Africa. This diamond mine in Angola is one of many in this region.

Zimbabwe and South Africa both mine gold. However the industry is much larger in South Africa where Johannesburg is the world's gold mining centre.

Mining for other elements is widespread, particularly in South Africa where platinum, ura-nium and coal are produced. However, the recycling of metals such as aluminium and steel is now becoming common throughout the world. This saves energy and resources but is reducing the demand for some minerals and so also diminishing their value.

The wildlife of southern Africa

A huge variety of wildlife is found in southern Africa. In the grasslands of South Africa the many species of antelope, such as the eland and oryx, are hunted by lions and cheetah. Huge herds of wildebeest roam the plains, and groups of giraffe and elephants wander around the waterholes. Leopards live in mountainous regions including those in Malawi and Zimbabwe. In the Okavango Swamp in Botswana, hippopotamus and crocodiles are abundant.

Madagascar is separated from mainland Africa by a considerable distance which has caused the animals there to evolve independently. A great number of species are unique to the island, including many varieties of the monkey-like lemur.

1. HYENA
2. CHIMPANZEE
3. AARDVARK
4. LEMUR

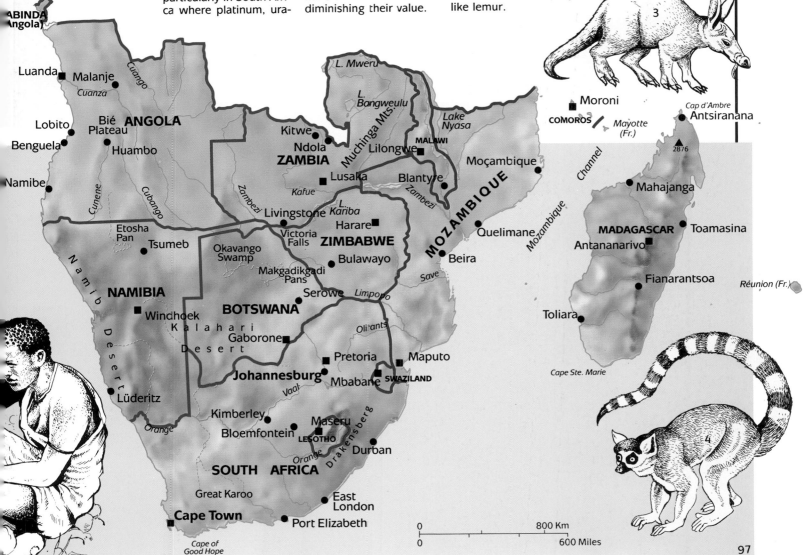

OCEANIA

Oceania is the name given to the region which includes Australia, New Zealand and the islands which are scattered across the Pacific Ocean. These islands are grouped into three areas: Melanesia, Micronesia and Polynesia. No-one knows exactly how many Pacific islands there are, but it is estimated that the total lies between twenty and 30 thousand. Some are coral islands while others, such as Hawaii, are volcanoes rising above the sea.

One of Australia's most famous attractions lies not on the land but in the sea. It is the beautiful Great Barrier Reef, which stretches for 2000 kilometres off the north-east coast. Farther south New Zealand's two main islands have a cooler, wetter climate than Australia, and a landscape which varies from rugged mountains to rolling, green plains.

Oceania
Highest point Mount Wilhelm (Papua New Guinea) 4508m. (14,790ft.)
Lowest point Lake Eyre (Australia) 16m. (52ft.) below sea level
Longest river Murray-Darling (Australia) 3718km. (2310 miles)
Largest lake Lake Eyre (Australia) 9300 sq. km. (3600 sq. miles)

AUSTRALIA
Area 7,682,300 sq. km. (2,966,151 sq. miles)
Population 18,967,000
Capital Canberra (pop. 347,000)
Currency Australian dollar
Official language(s) English
Chief products Sheep, beef cattle, cereal, fruit, wine, wool, minerals, salt, coal, bauxite, wheat
Exports Wool, lamb, beef, cereals, dairy products, machinery, minerals, tobacco
Imports Alcoholic drinks, coal, oil, food, machinery
AUSTRALIAN STATES AND TERRITORIES
New South Wales
Area 801,600 sq. km. (309,500 sq. miles)
Population 6,039,000
Capital Sydney (pop. 3,935,000)
Victoria
Area 227,600 sq. km. (87,800 sq. miles)
Population 4,373,000

Capital: Melbourne (pop. 3,321,000)
Queensland
Area 1,727,200 sq. km. (666,875 sq. miles)
Population 3,369,000
Capital Brisbane (pop. 1,548,000)
South Australia
Area 984,000 sq. km. (380,000 sq. miles)
Population 1,428,000
Capital Adelaide (pop. 1,083,000)
Western Australia
Area 2,525,500 sq. km. (975,000 sq. miles)
Population 1,726,000
Capital Perth (pop. 1,319,000)
Tasmania
Area 67,800 sq. km. (26,180 sq. miles)
Population: 459,000
Capital: Hobart (pop. 195,000)
Northern Territory
Area 1,346,200 sq. km. (520,000 sq. miles)
Population: 195,000
Capital: Darwin (pop. 84,000)
Australian Capital Territory
Area 2400 sq. km. (927 sq. miles)
Population: 299,000
Capital: Canberra

NEW ZEALAND
Area 267,844 sq. km. (103,415 sq. miles)
Population 3,811,000
Capital Wellington (pop. 335,000)
Largest cities Auckland (998,000)
Christchurch (331,000)
Hamilton (159,000)
Dunedin (112,000)
Currency New Zealand Dollar
Official language(s) English and Maori
Chief products Sheep, wool, lamb, beef and dairy cattle, hardwood timber, minerals (especially coal, iron, sand), wheat, poultry, natural gas
Exports Iron ore, wheat, wool, live sheep and lambs, oil, oil products, beef, butter, kiwi fruit
Imports Machinery, electrical equipment, vehicles, iron and steel, textiles

PAPUA NEW GUINEA
Area 462,840 sq. km. (178,655 sq. miles)
Population 4,705,000
Capital Port Moresby
Official language(s) English (Pidgin English and Hiri Motu are also spoken)
Chief products Copper, silver, gold, minerals, oil and gas, paint, plywood, cocoa, copra, tea, coffee

FIJI
Official name Matanitu Ko Fiti
Area 18,330 sq. km. (7075 sq. miles)
Population 801,000
Capital Suva
Official language(s) English and Fijian
Chief products Sugar cane and molasses, coconuts, ginger, copra, fruit, fish, vegetables, rice, timber

Name	Area sq. km. (sq. miles)	Population	Capital
American Samoa	196 (76)	64,000	Pago Pago
Cook Islands (NZ)	293 (113)	19,000	Avarua
French Polynesia	3940 (1520)	231,000	Papeete
Guam (US)	549 (212)	152,000	Agaña
Kiribati	717 (277)	88,000	Tarawa
Marshall Islands, Rep. of the	180 (70)	51,000	Majuro
Federated States of Micronesia	701 (271)	116,000	Palikir
Nauru	21.3 (8.2)	10,600	Yaren
New Caledonia (Fr.)	22,139 (8548)	209,000	Noumea
Niue (NZ)	259 (100)	1700	Alofi
Norfolk Island (Aus.)	34.5 (13.3)	1900	Kingston
Northern Mariana Islands (US)	476 (184)	69,000	Saipan
Palau	488 (188)	19,000	Koror
Pitcairn Islands	4.6 (1.75)	42	–
Samoa	2840 (1095)	169,000	Apia
Solomon Islands	27,556 (10,640)	429,000	Honiara
Tonga	699 (270)	100,000	Nuku'alofa
Tuvalu	24.6 (9.5)	10,600	Funafuti
Vanuatu	14,763 (5700)	193,000	Port Vila
Wallis and Futuna Is. (Fr.)	274 (106)	15,000	Matâ'utu

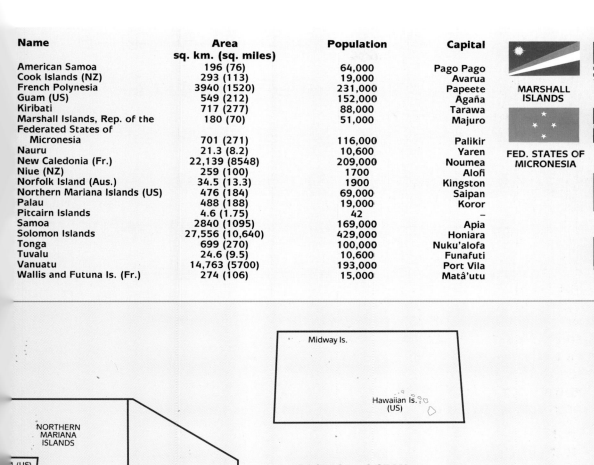

MARSHALL ISLANDS KIRIBATI TONGA
FED. STATES OF MICRONESIA NAURU TUVALU
PALAU VANUATU
SOLOMON IS. SAMOA

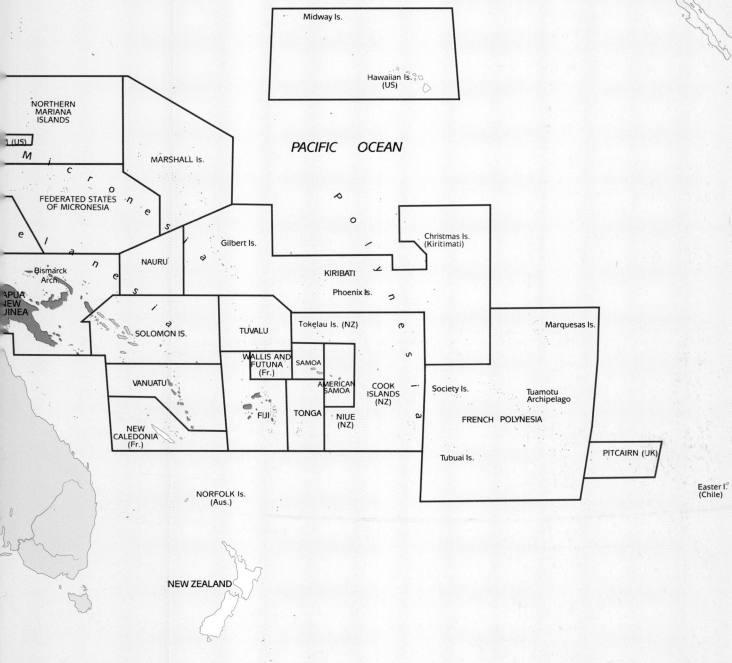

AUSTRALIA

Australia is made up of five mainland states, two mainland territories, the island state of Tasmania and seven external territories. The arid interior of the continent, known as the outback, is virtually uninhabited, but in areas where water can be found there are huge cattle stations and sheep farms – Australia is the world's largest producer of wool.

Eighty per cent of the Australian population lives in cities, almost all of which are located in the fertile area in the south-east between Adelaide and Brisbane, and around Perth in Western Australia. About 350,000 Aboriginal Australians, the native people of Australia, have survived. Some cling to their traditional ways of life, but most have moved to the cities, or live on lands set aside for them by the government.

Australia is one of the world's largest mineral producers – bauxite (aluminium ore), copper, iron ore and coal are all found in abundance in north and west Australia.

A sheep auction
Australia is the world's chief wool-producing country. Here, Merino sheep are being sold at an auction. The Merino is specially bred for its fine quality wool.

Ayers Rock
Ayers Rock is Australia's most famous landmark. It is three kilometres long and almost nine kilometres round. It lies in the middle of the vast flat desert lands of central Australia. The Rock is sacred to the Aboriginal people – inside it are caves with paintings and carvings on the walls which depict stories of their ancestors. It is known to the Aboriginal people as Uluru.

Surfing off Bondi beach
A surf lifesaver on one of the golden beaches near Sydney in south-eastern Australia. Beaches such as Bondi and Tamarama are only eight kilometres from the city centre.

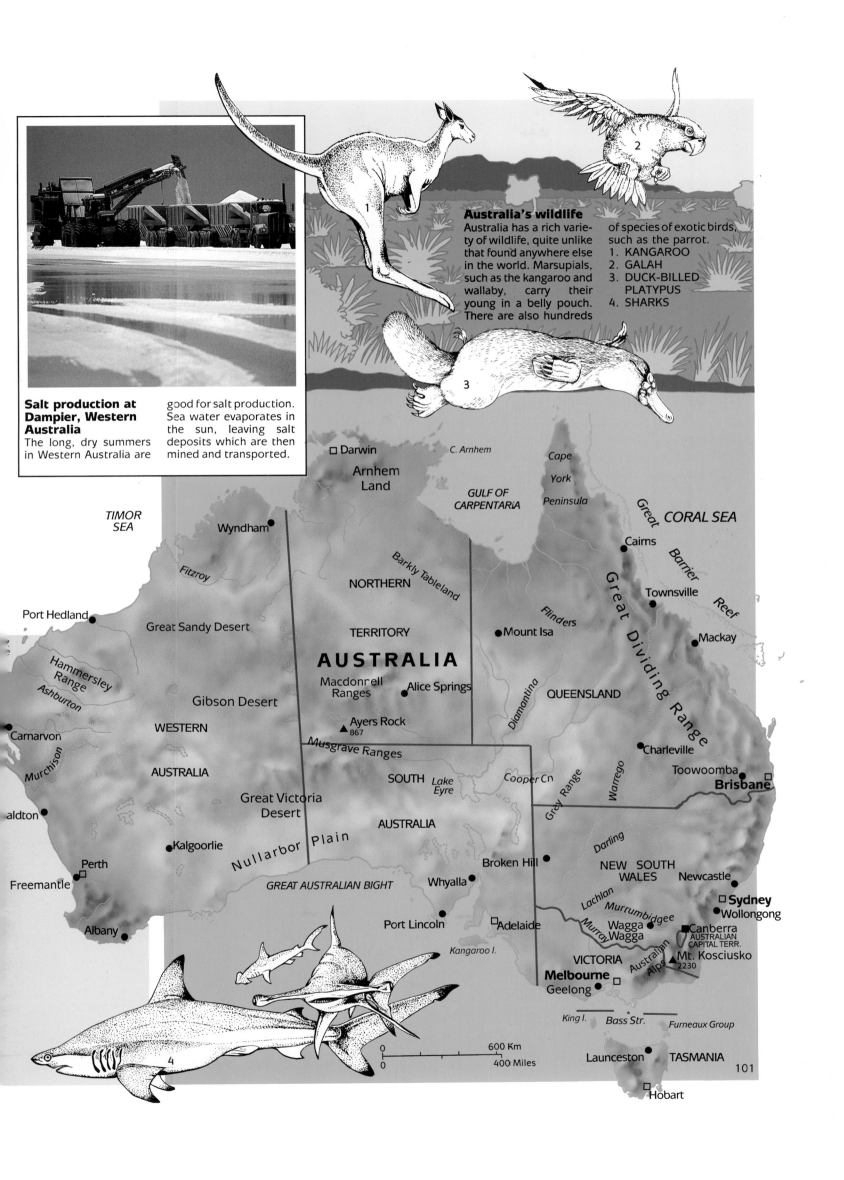

Salt production at Dampier, Western Australia
The long, dry summers in Western Australia are good for salt production. Sea water evaporates in the sun, leaving salt deposits which are then mined and transported.

Australia's wildlife
Australia has a rich variety of wildlife, quite unlike that found anywhere else in the world. Marsupials, such as the kangaroo and wallaby, carry their young in a belly pouch. There are also hundreds of species of exotic birds, such as the parrot.
1. KANGAROO
2. GALAH
3. DUCK-BILLED PLATYPUS
4. SHARKS

TIMOR SEA

□ Darwin
C. Arnhem
Arnhem Land
Cape York Peninsula
GULF OF CARPENTARIA
CORAL SEA
Great
Great Barrier Reef

Wyndham ●
Cairns ●
Fitzroy
Barkly Tableland
NORTHERN
Townsville ●
Port Hedland ●
Great Sandy Desert
TERRITORY
Mackay ●
Hammersley Range
Ashburton
Flinders
Mount Isa ●
Great Dividing Range
Carnarvon ●
Gibson Desert
AUSTRALIA
Macdonnell Ranges
Alice Springs ●
QUEENSLAND
Murchison
WESTERN
Diamantina
Ayers Rock ▲ 867
Charleville ●
aldton ●
AUSTRALIA
Musgrave Ranges
Toowoomba ●
Cooper Cn
Grey Range
Brisbane □
Kalgoorlie ●
SOUTH
Lake Eyre
Great Victoria Desert
AUSTRALIA
Warrego
Perth □
Nullarbor Plain
Darling
NEW SOUTH WALES
Newcastle ●
Freemantle ●
GREAT AUSTRALIAN BIGHT
Whyalla ●
Broken Hill ●
Lachlan
Murrumbidgee
Sydney □
Albany ●
Port Lincoln ●
□ Adelaide
Murray
Wagga Wagga
Canberra ■ AUSTRALIAN CAPITAL TERR.
Wollongong ●
Kangaroo I.
VICTORIA
Australian Alps
▲ Mt. Kosciusko 2230
Melbourne
Geelong ●
King I.
Bass Str.
Furneaux Group

600 Km
0
0
400 Miles
Launceston ●
TASMANIA
101
Hobart □

NEW ZEALAND

New Zealand consists of two large islands and a number of smaller ones. Parts of North Island are volcanically active, with bubbling mud pools and geysers which shoot boiling water up to 100 metres in the air. As well as being a tourist attraction, the geysers produce steam which is used to generate electricity. The lower mountain slopes and green plains on South Island provide ideal grazing land for sheep.

Most of the population of New Zealand lives on North Island and is descended from the Europeans who settled in the nineteenth and twentieth centuries. The native inhabitants of the country, the Maori, are now in the minority.

New Zealand's economy is based around agriculture – especially the export of dairy produce, meat and specialized food such as kiwi fruit. Recently, reserves of natural gas have been discovered off the west coast, and wood pulp and iron export industries have been established.

The Maori
Wood carving is a traditional craft of the Maori, the original inhabitants who came by canoe from other Pacific islands to New Zealand in about AD 800. The wood carvings, which show aspects of traditional Maori life, are mostly produced today for sale to tourists. Another traditional craft is the fashioning of jewellery, made from semi-precious stones and gems found on the islands.

Wellington
This is the port at Wellington, the capital of New Zealand, which is situated at the southern tip of North Island. It is characterized by steep hills, earthquakes and year-round gusting winds – its nickname is the 'windy city'. From the port, the Picton Ferry provides a link between North and South Islands. About sixty per cent of all exports, primarily dairy produce and lamb, is shipped in huge refrigerated containers from here to Europe, the USA and Japan. The remainder is transported from Auckland farther north.

Wildlife in New Zealand
New Zealand has a huge variety of animals and birds, many unique to the country, including the world's largest parrot, the kakapo.
1. KOTUKU (WHITE HERON)
2. KAKAPO
3. KIWI
4. FJORDLAND SKINK
5. FUR SEAL

North Cape

The Canterbury Plains
The Southern Alps rise high above the fertile Canterbury Plains on South Island. These plains, though small in area, are New Zealand's most important farming region. Here sheep are grazed and wheat, barley and potatoes are produced. New Zealand is the world's leading exporter of lamb and mutton.

The All Blacks
Many New Zealanders are enthusiastic supporters of rugby football. The All Blacks, so-called because of the colour of their kit, are the national team. Before play starts the All Blacks perform a traditional Maori dance.

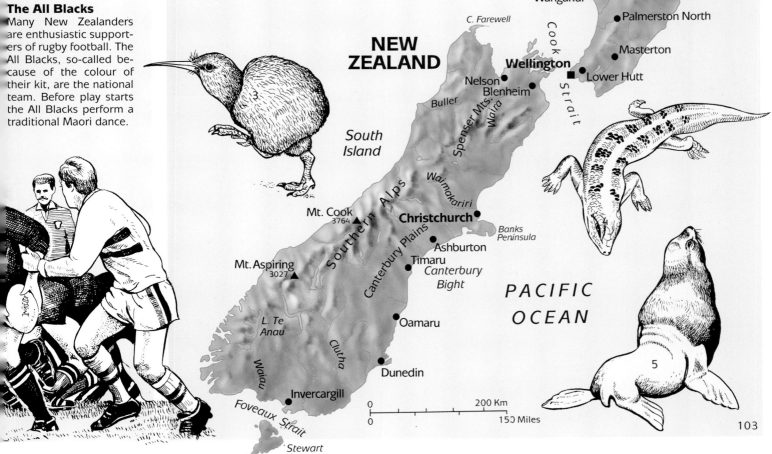

NEW ZEALAND

North Island

South Island

PACIFIC OCEAN

Whangarei
Great Barrier Island
Takapuna
Auckland
Manukau
Bay of Plenty
Hamilton
Tauranga
East Cape
Waipa
Waikato
Whakatane
Rotorua
Gisborne
New Plymouth
L. Taupo
Mahia Peninsula
Mt. Egmont 2518
Ruapehu 2796
Wanganui
Napier
Hastings
Wanganui
Palmerston North
C. Farewell
Masterton
Wellington
Lower Hutt
Nelson
Blenheim
Cook Strait
Buller
Waira
Spenser Mts.
Waimakariri
Mt. Cook 3764
Christchurch
Banks Peninsula
Ashburton
Mt. Aspiring 3027
Timaru
Canterbury Plains
Canterbury Bight
Southern Alps
L. Te Anau
Oamaru
Clutha
Waiau
Dunedin
Invercargill
Foveaux Strait
Stewart Island

0   200 Km
0   150 Miles

103

PACIFIC ISLANDS

The islands scattered across the Pacific Ocean, south-east of Asia, are grouped into three regions: Melanesia (which includes Papua New Guinea), Micronesia, and Polynesia which extends north to Hawaii and east to include Easter Island.

The original settlers of the islands are thought to have come by sea from south-east Asia. Today the Pacific islanders are still expert seafarers, and many of the smaller islands' economies rely on fishing. Much of the agriculture on the islands is subsistence farming. In the tropical climate yams, breadfruit, sweet potatoes and fruits are grown and sold in local markets. Larger islands such as Papua New Guinea also grow coffee, copra and cocoa for export. Valuable minerals reserves on some islands are an important source of income: New Caledonia is the third largest producer of nickel in the world, Christmas Island has large phosphate supplies, and copper is mined on Papua New Guinea.

South Sea paradise
This idyllic view near Bora Bora in the French Polynesian islands is typical of much of the scenery in the South Seas. The beauty of the surroundings and the tropical climate are attracting more and more visitors every year. Some islands are developing luxury resorts to encourage the extra revenue that tourism brings.

Modern ways
Until recently, many of the Pacific islands were undeveloped and the people lived as they had for thousands of years. Development of the islands by outsiders, has changed the traditional way of life dramatically. Younger people in particular have adopted many 'Western' ways.

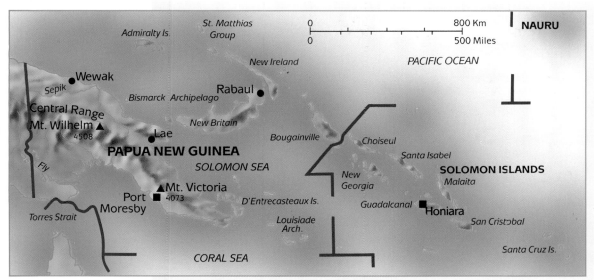

St. Matthias
Group
Admiralty Is.

0   800 Km
0   500 Miles

NAURU

New Ireland

PACIFIC OCEAN

Wewak
Sepik
Rabaul

Central Range
Mt. Wilhelm ▲
4508
Lae

Bismarck Archipelago
New Britain

Bougainville
Choiseul
Santa Isabel

SOLOMON ISLANDS

PAPUA NEW GUINEA

SOLOMON SEA

Fly

▲ Mt. Victoria
■ 4073
Port
Moresby

D'Entrecasteaux Is.

New
Georgia
Malaita

Guadalcanal
■ Honiara

San Cristobal

Torres Strait

Louisiade
Arch.

CORAL SEA

Santa Cruz Is.

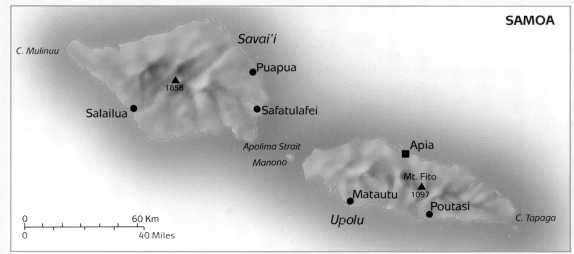

SAMOA

Savai'i

C. Mulinuu

Puapua
▲
1858
Safatulafei

Salailua

Apolima Strait
Manono

Apia ■

Mt. Fito
▲ 1097

Matautu
Poutasi

Upolu

C. Tapaga

0   60 Km
0   40 Miles

Coconut wealth
Copra, the dry white flesh of the coconut, being stored at Port Moresby Wharf in Papua New Guinea, ready for export. Copra brings wealth to many Pacific islands. It is prepared by removing the fibrous husk of the coconut, splitting the nut and laying out strips of the white 'meat' to dry in the sun. The meat is then crushed to extract the oil.

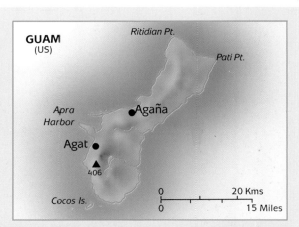

GUAM
(US)

Ritidian Pt.

Pati Pt.

Apra
Harbor

Agaña

Agat
▲
406

Cocos Is.

0   20 Kms
0   15 Miles

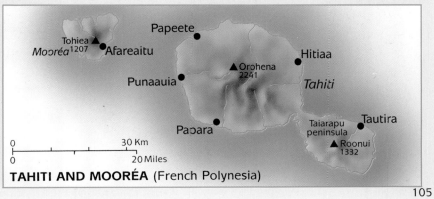

Papeete

Tohiea ▲
Mooréa 1207
Afareaitu

Hitiaa

▲ Orohena
2241

Tahiti

Punaauia

Papara

Taiarapu
peninsula
▲ Roonui
1332

Tautira

TAHITI AND MOORÉA (French Polynesia)

ARCTIC AND ANTARCTICA

The Arctic and Antarctica are remote, ice-bound regions around the two Poles. At the North Pole a layer of ice about six metres deep floats within the Arctic Ocean. At the South Pole the ice cap is on average 2300 metres thick over the buried land mass of Antarctica.

Both regions are extremely cold. However, during summer in the northern hemisphere the snow and ice melt in parts of the Arctic, and moss, lichen and flowers appear. About two million people live within the Arctic Circle, including the Inuit of Alaska and Greenland. No-one lives permanently in Antarctica, although scientists have set up camps there to study the environment.

The Arctic is rich in mineral resources including fossil fuels, diamonds and gold. These are being exploited by the surrounding countries. Antarctica is rich in food resources from the sea, but in accordance with international agreement, it has remained untouched so far.

Research in Antarctica

The first explorers reached Antarctica in the early part of this century. Today, researchers from many countries have set up stations in the inhospitable conditions, even growing their own vegetables in heated greenhouses. Thirty-nine nations are party

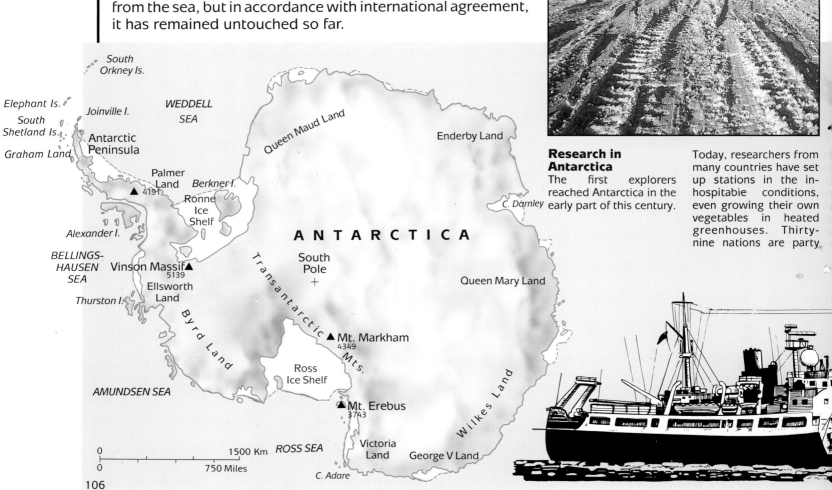

South Orkney Is.

Elephant Is.
South Shetland Is.
Graham Land
Joinville I.
WEDDELL SEA
Antarctic Peninsula
Palmer Land
▲ 4191
Berkner I.
Ronne Ice Shelf
Queen Maud Land
Enderby Land
C. Darnley

Alexander I.

BELLINGS- HAUSEN SEA
Vinson Massif ▲
5139
Ellsworth Land
ANTARCTICA
South Pole
+
Queen Mary Land

Thurston I.

Byrd Land
Transantarctic Mts.
▲ Mt. Markham
4349
Ross Ice Shelf
Wilkes Land

AMUNDSEN SEA

▲ Mt. Erebus
3743

0 — 1500 Km
0 — 750 Miles
ROSS SEA
Victoria Land
George V Land
C. Adare

106

Animals in the cold

The Poles and the surrounding seas support a huge variety of wildlife, despite the extreme cold.

1. ARCTIC SKUA
2. POLAR BEAR
3. WALRUS
4. KILLER WHALE

...to agreements made in 1961 and 1991 to demilitarize the area, ban mineral exploitation, assure international scientific cooperation, and provide environmental protection.

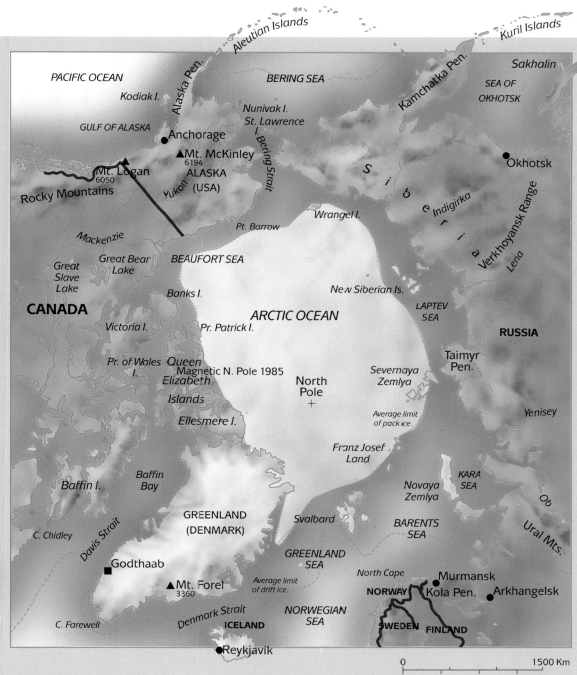

PACIFIC OCEAN
Aleutian Islands
Kuril Islands
BERING SEA
Kamchatka Pen.
Sakhalin
SEA OF OKHOTSK
Kodiak I.
Nunivak I.
St. Lawrence I.
GULF OF ALASKA
Anchorage
Alaska Pen.
Bering Strait
Okhotsk
▲Mt. McKinley
6194
Mt. Logan
6050
ALASKA
(USA)
Rocky Mountains
Yukon
Siberia
Indigirka
Verkhoyansk Range
Lena
Pt. Barrow
Wrangel I.
Mackenzie
Great Bear Lake
BEAUFORT SEA
New Siberian Is.
LAPTEV SEA
Great Slave Lake
Banks I.
ARCTIC OCEAN
Taimyr Pen.
RUSSIA
CANADA
Victoria I.
Pr. Patrick I.
Severnaya Zemlya
Yenisey
Pr. of Wales I.
Queen
Elizabeth
Islands
Magnetic N. Pole 1985
North Pole
+
Average limit of pack ice.
Ellesmere I.
Franz Josef Land
KARA SEA
Baffin I.
Baffin Bay
Novaya Zemlya
Ob
GREENLAND (DENMARK)
Svalbard
BARENTS SEA
Ural Mts.
C. Chidley
Davis Strait
Godthaab
North Cape
Murmansk
Mt. Forel
3360
Average limit of drift ice.
GREENLAND SEA
NORWAY
Kola Pen.
Arkhangelsk
C. Farewell
Denmark Strait
ICELAND
NORWEGIAN SEA
SWEDEN
FINLAND
Reykjavik

| 0 | | 1500 Km |
| 0 | | 750 Miles |

Dying traditions

The ancestors of these Inuit children lived in isolated communities in the Arctic, and survived by hunting and fishing. They caught caribou and reindeer, which provided them with meat, and skins for making clothes and tents. When they moved on to search for food, teams of dogs pulled the sledges.

Today the Arctic is no longer so isolated. Since the discovery of oil, mining communities have sprung up and with them schools, shops and hospitals. The traditional way of life has been destroyed and most of the Inuit now live in permanent homes in these mining communities.

GENERAL INDEX

Page numbers in *italics* refer to illustrations

A

Abu Dhabi *78*, 79
Afghanistan 74, 75, 80
Africa: 90–7; agriculture 20, 92, 93, 94, 95; animals 13; climate 11; nations 15; languages 19; minerals 23; oil 92, 94; population 17; religions 19; vegetation 10
agriculture 20–1; Africa 92, 94, 95, 96; America 20, 58, 66, 68, 70; Asia 50, 74, 78, 82, 84, 87, 89; Europe 24, 28, 30, 32, 34, 35, 44, 45, 46, 47, 50; Oceania 103, 104
Alaska 12, 56, 57
Albania 24, 27, 44, 45
Alps (mts.) 24, 26, 38
Amazon, R. 12, 64, 68, 69
America *see* North America; South America
Andalusia 42, *42*
Andes (mts.) 12, 64, *64*, 66, *66*
animals 12–13
Antarctica 16, 106–7
apartheid 96
Arctic 106–7, *107*
Argentina 64, 70, 71
Asia: 72–89; agriculture 20, 21, 50, 74, 78, 82, 84, 87, 89; animals 13; climate 11; nations 15; languages 19; minerals 22, 23; oil 50, 78, 79, *79*, 80, 84, 86; religions 19; vegetation 10
Atacama Desert 64, 70
Atomium (Brussels) *34*, 35
Australia 11, 13, 15, 19, 23, 98, 100–1
Austria 24, 26, 27, 38, 39
Ayers Rock 100, *100*

B

Balinese dancers 85, *85*
Balkan Mts. 26
ballet, Russian 51, *51*
bananas *60*, 61, 66
Bangladesh 73, 82, 83
banking 30, 38, 40, 58
barley 20
Basque movement 43
Belgium 24, 34, 35
Berlin 36, 37, *36–7*
Bilbao 43, *43*
Blanc, Mont 26
Bolivia 64, 66, *66*
Bora Bora 104, *104*
Bosnia and Hercegovina 14, 27, 44, 45
Botswana 91, 96
Brandenburg Gate *36–7*, 37
Brasilia 68
Brazil 64, 68–9
British Isles 30–1
Bryce Canyon 56, *56*
Buddhism 19, 82, 85, 86
Buenos Aires 70, 71, *71*
Bulgaria 27, 44, 45
bull-fighting 42, *42*

C

cacti 61, *61*
California 58, *58*
Canada 10, 12, 52, 54–5
canals 29, 34, 54, *54*, 86, *86*
Caribbean Is. 23, 62–3
cars *see* motor vehicles
cattle herding 29, 80, 95
cereal crops 20, 26, 30, 32, 46, 50, 54, 56, 70, 76, 82
chemical industry 34, 35, 42, 45, 67
Chile 64, *64*, 70, 71, *71*

Chiloe, I. 70, *70*
China 13, 15, 16, 18, 19, 21, 23, 72, 86–7
Christianity 19, 40, 48, 67, 76
climate, world 10–11
coal 22, 30, 36, *36*, 46, 50, 66, 86, 96, 97, 100, 106
cocoa 94, 104
coffee 21, 62, 66, 68, 84, 94, 104
Colombia 64, 66
Commonwealth of Independent States (CIS) 20, 22, 23, 48
copper 22, 23, 70, 100, 104
copra 104, 105, *105*
corn *see* cereal crops
cotton 21, 22, 76, *76*, 82
Croatia 14, 27, 44, 45
Curaçao (I.) 63, *63*
Czech Republic 14, 27, 46

D

dairy farming 26, 30, 34, 35, 102
Danube, R. 26, 44, 45
Denmark 24, 28
deserts 10, 13, 54, 78, 90, 92
diamonds 22, 23, 96, 97, *97*, 106
Dinka tribe 92, 92–3
Dolomites (mts.) 24, 41, *41*

E

Earth 6–7
Ecuador 64, 66
Egypt 90, 92
El Salvador 52, 60
electronics industries 22, 28, 30, 36, 88, 89
Empty Quarter 74, 78, *78*
engineering 28, 30, 32, 34, 36, 37, 88
England 30, 31
Eritrea 91, 93
Estonia 26, 51
Ethiopia 90, 92, 93
Europe: 24–51; agriculture 20, 21, 26, 28, 30, 32, 34, 35, 44, 45, 47; animals 13; climate 11; European Union 15, 27; languages 19; minerals 22, 23; nations 15; oil 28, 31, 45, 46; population 16, 17; religions 19

F

famine *see* food supplies, world
farming *see* agriculture
festivals 39, 46, 62, *62*, 68, 85, 88, 93
Finland 25, 28, 29
fishing 28, 54, 63, 88, 94, *94*, 104
floods 83, *83*
food supplies, world 16, 17, 92, 93
football 70, *70*
forests 10, 52, 64, 68, 69, 90, 94
France 15, 24, 26, 27, 32–3
fruit 26, 40, 42, 44, 58, 61, 62, 68, 76, 77, 92, 102, 104

G

Ganges, R. 72, 82, *82*, 83
gardens, Japanese 88, *88*
gauchos 70, *70*
Germany 24, 26, 27, 36–7
geysers 28, 102
gold 22, 23, 46, 60, 66, 97, 106
grapes 21, *see also* wine

grasslands 10, 54, 56, 90, *90*
Great Barrier Reef 98
Great Lakes 54, 58
Great Rift Valley 90, 94
Greece 26, 44
Gulf, Persian 74, 80
Gulf Stream 30, 32, 35

H

Himalayas (mts.) 13, 72, *72*, 74, 82
Hinduism 19, 82
Holland *see* Netherlands
Horn, Cape 64, 71
Hungary 27, 46, 47
hydroelectric power 38, 50

I

ice hockey 54, *54*
Iceland 25, 28, 29
India 13, 16, 19, 21, 72, 82, 83
Indians, American 58, *58*, 60, *60*, 66, *66*, 69, *69*, 70
Indonesia 72, 84
Inuits 106, 107, *107*
Iran 74, 80, 81
Iraq 75, 80
Ireland 25, 27, 30, *30*
iron 22, 23, 28, 36, 43, 58, 66, 68, 86, 100, 102
irrigation 50, 76, 77, 78, 80, 82, 92
Islam 19, 78, 79, 80, 81, 82
Israel 74, 76, 77
Italy 24, 25, 26, 27, 40–1

J

Japan 19, 79, 88–9
jazz 59, *59*
Jerusalem 74, *74*
Jews 19, 58, 76, *76*
Jordan 75, 76, 77

K

Kazakhstan 50, 73
Kenya 90, 94, 95
kibbutz 77, *77*
Kilimanjaro (mt.) 90
Kuwait 75, 80
Kyrgyzstan 49, *49*, 73

L

Lagos 94, *94*
languages, world 18–19
Lebanon 75, 76
Libya 90, 92
Lloyds Building (London) 30, *30*
logging 28, *28*, 54, 55
London 30
Louvre 32, *32*
lumber *see* logging
Luxembourg 27, 34

M

Macedonia 14, 27, 44, 45
Malaysia 73, 84
Mandela, Nelson 96
Maori 102, *102*
Maracaibo, L. 67, *67*
Mardi Gras 59, 68, *68*
markets *34*, 35, 44, *44*, 51, 60, 63, 78, 82, 93
Marsh Arabs 80, *80*
Masai tribe 94, 95, *95*
Mecca 78, 81
Melanesia 98, 104
Meteora 44, *44*
Mexico 52, 60, 61
Micronesia 98, 99, 104
millet 20
mineral wealth, world 22–3
monasteries 44, 77
Mongolia 72, 73

monsoons 82
Morocco 90, 93
Moscow 48, *48*, 50, *50*
mosques *78*, 79
motor vehicles 22, 28, 30, 32, 40, 58, 88, 94
Muslims *see* Islam

N

Namibia 91, 96, *96*
Nepal 72, 73
Netherlands 24, 27, 34, 35
New Caledonia 99, 104
New England 59, *59*
New Zealand 13, 98, 102–3
Newfoundland 54
Nicaragua 52, 60
nickel 22, 23, 54, 104
Nigeria 94
Nile, R. 92, *92*
North America: 52–63; agriculture 20, 58; animals 13; climate 10, 11; minerals 22, 23; nations 14; oil 56, 57, 60; population 16; religions 19
North Pole 10, 106
Northern Ireland 30
Norway 25, 28, 29

O

Oceania: 98–105; agriculture 102, 103, 104; animals 13
oil 22, 23; Africa 92, 94; America 56, 57, 60, 67, 70; Arabian peninsula 74, 78, 79; Asia 50, 80, 84, 86; Europe 28, 31, 45, 46
olives 26, 42, *42*, 44, 76
Oporto 42, *42*

P

Pakistan 72, 82
Palestinians 76
Pampas 64, 70
Panama Canal 61, *61*
paper 28
Papua New Guinea 98, 104, 105
Paraguay 65, 70
Paris 32, *32*
Persepolis 81, *81*
Persian carpets 80, *80*
Persian Gulf 74, 79
Peru 65, 66, 67
Petra 77, *77*
Poland 26, 46, 47, *47*
polar regions 10, 12, 16, 106–7
Polynesia 98, 104
population, world 16–17
Portugal 25, 27, 42
Potala Palace (Lhasa) 86, *86*
Prague 46, *46*
prairies *see* grasslands
Pyrenees (mts.) 24

R

railways 33, *33*, 50, *50*
rainfall, world 11
rainforests 10, 12, 52, 64, 68, *68*, 69, 90, 94
religions, world 18–19
Rhine, R. 26, 36
rice 20, 82, 84, 86, 89
Rocky Mts. 52, 55, *55*
Romania 26, 45
Rothenburg 36, *36*
Rotterdam 35, *35*
rubber 21, 84
rugby football 103, *103*
Russian 48, 49, 50, 51

S

Sahara desert 90, 92
St. Lawrence Seaway 54
St. Petersburg 50, *50*
salt 76, 101, *101*
Salzburg 39, *39*
Sami 29, *29*

San people 96, *96*
Saudi Arabia 74, 78
savanna 10, 90, 96, 97
Scotland 30, 31
seasons 7, *7*
sheep 30, 70, 100, *100*, 102, 103
sherry 42
shipping 22, 30, 35, 42, 43, 44, 46, 50, 74, 88
Sikhism 19
silver 22, 23, 60, 66
Singapore 72, 84
skiing 32, 38, 39, *39*, 41
Slovakia 14, 26, 27, 46, 47
Slovenia 14, 27, 44, 45
sorghum 20
South Africa 91, 96, 97
South America: 64–71; agriculture 20, 66, 68, 70; animals 12; climate 10, 11; languages 18; minerals 22, 23; nations 14; oil 67, 70; population 16; religions 19
Southern Alps 103, *103*
Spain 24, 25, 27, 42, 43
spices 82, *82*
steel 22, 30, 32, 42, 43, 46, 50, 52, 94
steppes *see* grasslands
Sudan 90, 92, 93
sugar 46, 60, 62, *62*, 84
Sun 6, *6*, 7, *7*, 19
Sweden 25, 28
Switzerland 24, 26, 27, 38, 39
Syria 75, 76

T

Tanzania 90, 91, 94
tea 21, 86, 89, *89*, 94
temperatures, world 11
textiles 30, 34, 40, 42, 60, 70, 76, *76*, 82, 86
TGV 33, *33*
Thailand 73, 84
Tibet 72
tin 22, 23, 66, 84, *84*
Titicaca, L. 66, *66*
tobacco 32, 62, 76
tourism 28, 32, 36, 38, 41, 42, 44, 62, 85
transport 29, 33, 50, 78, 80, 86
tundra 10
Turkey 74, 76, *76*

U

Ukraine 27, 50
United Arab Emirates 75, 79
United Kingdom 15, 24, 27, 30–1
United Nations 15, 38
United States of America 6, 10, 15, 16, 23, 52, 56–9
Urals (mts.) 24, 48
uranium 22, 23, 46, 54, 97
Uruguay 65, 70

V

Vatican City 24, 26, 40, *40*
vegetation 10–11
Venezuela 65, 66, 67
Venice *40–1*, 41
volcanoes 28, 52, 71, 72, 88, 98

W

Wales 30, 31
Wellington 102, *102*
weaving 60, *60*
West Indies 52
wheat *see* cereal crops
whisky 30, 31
wildlife, world 12–13
wine 21, 26, 32, 33, 40, 42, 58
wool 22, 66, 70, 100

Y

Yemen 75, 78
Yugoslavia 27, 44

108

MAP INDEX

Page numbers in **bold** refer to entries in information files

A

Abadan 81
Aberdeen 31
Abu Dhabi **75**, 79
Abuja **90**, 95
Acapulco 61
Accra **90**, 95
Aconcagua (mt.) **64**, 71
Adana **74**, 77
Addis Ababa **90**, 93
Adelaide **10**, 11, **98**, 101
Aden 79
Adriatic Sea 41, 45
Aegean Sea 45
Afghanistan 15, 73, 75, **75**, 81
Africa **8**, 9, 11, 13, 15, 17, 19, 21, 23, 90-7
Agaña **99**, 105
Ahmadabad 83
Ajaccio 33
Akureyri 29
Alabama 57, **59**
Åland 29
Alaska 14, 53, 57, **59**, 107
Albacete 43
Albania 15, 25, **27**, 45
Albany (Aust.) 101
Albany (N.Y.) 57, 59
Albert, L. 47
Alberta 54–5
Ålborg **24**, 29
Albuquerque 57, **59**
Aleppo 77
Aleutian Is. 57, 107
Alexandria 93
Algarve 43
Algeria **14**, 15, 23, **90**, 91, 92–3
Algiers **90**, 93
Alicante 43
Alice Springs 101
Alkmaar 35
Almaty **48**, **51**, **73**
Almería 43
Alps (mts.) 9, 33, 37, 39
Altiplano 67
Amazon, R. 9, **9**, **64**, 69
Amiens 33
Amman **75**, 77
Amritsar 83
Amsterdam **24**, 35
Amur, R. 9, **9**, 49, 87
Anatolia 77
Anchorage 57, 107
Ancona 41
Andalusia 43
Andaman Is. 83, 84
Andes (mts.) 8, **8**, 65, 67, 71
Andorra **14**, 15, 25, **26**, 43
Anglesey, I. of 31
Angola 15, 23, 91, **91**, 97
Anguilla **53**, 63
Ankara **74**, 77
Annapolis 57, **59**
Antananarivo **91**, 97
Antarctica **8**, 107
Antigua and Barbuda **14**, 53, **53**, 63
Antilles 62–3
Antofagasta 71
Antwerp **24**, 35
Apeldoorn 35
Appennines (mts.) 41
Apia **99**, 105
Appalachian Mts. 57
Arabia **9**
Arabian Sea 83
Aral Sea **9**, 48
Ararat, Mt. 77
Arctic Ocean 9, **9**, 49, 107
Ardennes 35
Arequipa **65** 67
Argentina **14**, **14**, **20**, 21, 22, **64**, 65, 71
Århus **24**, 29
Arizona **56**, **59**

Arkansas 57, **59**
Arkhangelsk 48, 107
Armenia 15, 25, **26**, 48, 51
Arnhem 35
Arnhem Land 101
Aruba **53**, 63
Ashgabat **48**, **51**, **73**
Asia **8**, 9, 11, 13, 15, 17, 19, 21, 23, 72–89
Asmara 93
Assam 83
Astrakhan 48
Asunción **65**, 71
Aswan 93
Atacama Desert **8**, 67, 71
Athens **26**, 45
Atlanta 57, **59**
Atlantic Ocean 8-9, **9**
Atlas Mts. 92-3
Auckland **98**, 103
Augsburg 37
Augusta 57, **59**
Austin 33, **35**, 41, 57, **59**
Australia 9, **9**, 13, **14**, 15, 17, 19, **20**, 21, 23, **23**, 98 **98**, 100–1
Australian Alps 101
Austria 15, 25, **27**, 38–9
Avignon 33
Ayers Rock 101
Azerbaijan 25, **26**, 48, **51**

B

Badajoz 43
Baffin I. **9**, 55, 107
Baghdad **75**, 81
Bahamas 14, 53, **53**, 63
Bahia Blanca 71
Bahrain **10**, 11, 73, 75, **75**, 79
Bakhtaran **74**, 81
Baku **26**, 48, **51**
Balaton, L. 47
Balearic Is. 43
Baltic Sea 29, 37, 47, 48
Baltimore 57
Bamako **91**, 92
Bandar Abbas 81
Bandar Seri Begawan 85
Bandung 84
Bangalore **16**, 83
Bangkok **16**, 17, **73**, 84
Bangladesh 14, 15, **20**, **73**, 83
Bangui **91**, 95
Banja Luka 45
Banjul **91**, 94
Banks I. 54, 107
Barbados **14**, 53, **53**, 63
Barcelona **25**, 43
Barents Sea 107
Bari 41
Barrow 10, **10**
Basel 39
Basra 81
Basse-Terre **53**, 63
Bastia 33
Bath 31
Baton Rouge 57, **59**
Bavaria 37
Baykal, L. 49
Bayonne 33
Beijing (Peking) **16**, 17, **72**, 87
Beira 97
Beirut **75**, 77
Belarus 25, **26**, 48, **51**
Belém 69
Belfast 31
Belgium 15, **24**, 25, **27**, 35
Belgrade **27**, 45
Belize 14, 53, **53**, 61
Belmopan **53**, 61
Belo Horizonte **64**, 69
Ben Nevis (mt.) 31
Bengal, Bay of 83
Benghazi 93
Benguela 97

Benin 15, 91, **91**, 95
Bergen 29
Bering Sea 49, 57, 107
Berlin **26**, 37
Bermuda 53, **53**, 63
Bern **27**, 39
Bhutan 15, **72**, 73, 83
Bialystok 47
Bielefeld 37
Bilbao 43
Birmingham (UK) **24**, 31
Birmingham (US) 57
Biscay, Bay of 33
Bishkek **48**, **51**, **73**
Bismarck 57, **59**
Bissau **91**, 94
Black Forest 37
Black Sea 45, 48, 77
Blackpool 31
Blanc, Mt. 33, 41
Blantyre 97
Bloemfontein 97
Bogotá **64**, 67
Bohemia 47
Boise 56, **59**
Bolivia 14, 22, **23**, **64**, 65, 67
Bologna 41
Bolzano 41
Bonn **26**, 37
Bordeaux **25**, 33
Borneo **9**, 85
Bornholm 29
Bosnia and Hercegovina 15, 25, **27**, 45
Bosporus 77
Boston 57, 59
Bothnia, Gulf of 29
Botswana 15, 23, 91, **91**, 97
Boulogne 33
Bourges 33
Bournemouth 31
Bradford 31
Brahmaputra, R. 83
Brasília **64**, 69
Braşov 45
Bratislava **27**, 47
Brazil 14, **14**, **20**, 21, 22, **22**, **23**, **64**, 65, 69
Brazzaville **91**, 95
Breda 35
Bremen 37
Brenner Pass 39
Brescia 41
Brest 33
Brighton 31
Brindisi 41
Brisbane **98**, 101
Bristol 31
British Columbia 54
Brittany 33
Brno 47
Broken Hill 101
Bruges **24**, 35
Brunei 15, **72**, 73, 85
Brussels **10**, 11, **24**, 35
Bucharest **26**, 45
Budapest **27**, 47
Buenos Aires **16**, 17, **64**, 71
Buffalo 57
Bujumbura **91**, 95
Bulawayo 97
Bulgaria 15, 23, 25, **27**, 45
Burgas 45
Burgos 43
Burgundy 33
Burkina Faso 15, 91, **91**, 94–5
Burma *see* Myanmar
Bursa **74**, 77
Burundi 15, 91, **91**, 95

C

Cabinda 97
Cádiz 43
Cagliari 41
Caicos Is. **53**, 63
Cairns 101

Cairo **16**, 17, **90**, 93
Calgary **52**, 54
Cali 67
Calicut 83
California 56, **59**
California, Gulf of 60
Cambodia 15, 73, **73**, 84
Cambrian Mts. 31
Cambridge 31
Cameroon 15, **90**, 91, 95
Canada 14, **14**, **20**, 21, 22, **22**, **23**, **52**, 53, 54–5, 107
Canary Is. 43, 91, 92
Canberra **98**, 101
Cannes 33
Cantabrian Mts. 43
Canterbury Plains 103
Cape Town **91**, 97
Cape Verde 91, **91**, 94
Cape York Peninsula 101
Caracas **65**, 67
Cardiff 31
Caribbean Sea 62–3
Carlisle 31
Cárnarvon 101
Carpathian Mts. 45, 47
Carson City 56, 59
Cartagena (Colombia) 67
Cartagena (Spain) 43
Casablanca 92
Caspian Sea **9**, **25**, 48, **72**
Castile 43
Catalonia 43
Catania 41
Catanzaro 41
Caucasus Mts. 48
Cayenne **65**, 67
Cayman Is. **53**, 62
Central African Republic 15, 91, **91**, 95
Central America 8, **8**, 10, 11, 14, 16, 17, 18, 19, 20, 22, 53, 60–1
Chad 15, 91, **91**, 93
Chad, L. 93
Champagne 33
Chang *see* Yangtze
Channel Is. 31
Charleroi **24**, 35
Charleston 57, **59**
Charlotte 57
Charlottetown 55
Chattahoochee, R. 41
Chennai (Madras) **16**, 17, **72**, 83
Chengdu 87
Cherbourg 33
Cheyenne 57, **59**
Chiang Mai 84
Chicago **52**, 57
Chiclayo **65**, 67
Chile 14, 22, **23**, **64**, 65, 71
Chiloé 71
China **14**, 15, **20**, 21, 22, 23, **23**, **72**, 73, 98–9
Chişinău **26**, 48, **51**
Chittagong 83
Chongqing 87
Christchurch **98**, 103
Churchill 55
Cincinnati 57
Ciudad Bolivar 67
Ciudad Real 43
Clermont Ferrand 33
Cleveland 57
Coimbra 43
Cologne 37
Colombia 14, **64**, 65, 67
Colombo **72**, 83
Colorado 57, **59**
Colorado, R. 56–7
Columbia 57, **59**
Columbus 57, **59**
Como, L. 41
Comodoro Rivadavia 71
Comoros Is. 15, 91, **91**, 97
Conakry **91**, 94
Concepción 71
Concord 57, **59**
Congo, R. 9, **9**, 95
Connecticut 57, **59**
Constance, L. 37, 39
Constanţa 45
Constantine 93
Cook Is. 99, **99**

Cook, Mt. 103
Copenhagen **24**, 29
Coral Sea 101, 105
Córdoba (Argentina) **64**, 71
Córdoba (Spain) 43
Corfu 45
Cork 31
Corrientes **64**, 71
Corsica 33
Cosenza 41
Costa Rica 14, **52**, 53, 61
Côte d'Ivoire 15, **90**, 91, 94
Cottbus 37
Coventry 31
Crete 45
Crimea 48
Croatia 15, 25, **27**, 45
Cuba 14, 22, 53, **53**, 62–3
Curaçao 63
Cuzco 67
Cyclades 45
Cyprus 15, 25, **26**, 75, 77, 87, 89
Czech Republic 15, 23, 25, **27**, 47

D

Dakar **91**, 94
Dallas **52**, 57
Damascus **75**, 77
Damman **74**, 79
Danube, R. 9, 37, 39, 45, 47
Dar es Salaam 95
Darling, R. **98**, 101
Darwin **98**, 101
Dasht-e-Kavir 81
Davao 85
Dawson 54
Dead Sea **72**, 77
Death Valley **52**
Debrecen 47
Deccan (plateau) 83
Delaware 57, **59**
Delhi **72**, 83
Democratic Republic of Congo 15, 23, **90**, 91, 95
Den Helder 35
Denmark 15, 22, **24**, 25, **27**, 29
Denver 57, **59**
Des Moines 57, **59**
Detroit **52**, 57
Devon I. 55
Dhaka 16, 17, **73**, 83
Dhaulagiri, Mt. **9**, 83
Dijon 33
Djibouti 15, **90**, 91, **91**, 93
Dnepropetrovsk 48
Dnieper, R. 48
Dodoma **91**, 95
Doha **75**, 79
Dolomites (mts.) 41
Dominica 53, **53**, 63
Dominican Republic 14, 22, 53, **53**, 63
Don, R. 48
Donetsk 48
Dordogne, R. 33
Dordrecht 35
Dortmund 37
Douala 9
Douro, R. 43
Dover (UK) 31
Dover (US) 57, **59**
Drakensberg (mts.) 97
Drammen 29
Dresden 37
Dubai 79
Dublin **25**, 31
Dubrovnik 45
Duisburg 37
Duluth 57
Dundee 31
Dunedin **98**, 103
Durban 97
Dushanbe 48, **51**, **73**
Düsseldorf 37

E

East China Sea 87
East London 97
Easter I. 99
Ecuador 14, **64**, 67
Edinburgh 31

Edmonton **52**, 54
Edward, L. 95
Egmont, Mt. 103
Egypt 15, **22**, 23, **90**, 91, 93
Eindhoven **24**, 35
El Aaiún **91**, 92
El Paso 57
El Salvador 14, **21**, **52**, 53, 61
Elba, I. 41
Elbe, R. 37
Elbert, Mt. 57
Elbrus, Mt. **25**, 48
Elburz Mts. 81
Elgon, Mt. 47
Ellesmere I. 55, 107
England 31
English Channel 31
Enschede 35
Enugu 95
Equatorial Guinea 15, 91, **91**, 95
Erciyaş, Mt. 77
Erebus, Mt. 106
Erfurt 37
Erie, L. 55, 57
Eritrea **91**, 93
Erzurum 77
Esbjerg **24**, 29
Esfahan **74**, 81
Essen 37
Estonia 25, **26**, 48, **51**
Ethiopia 15, **21**, **90**, 91, 93
Etna, Mt. 41
Euphrates, R. 77, 81
Europe **8**, 9, 11, 13, 15, 17, 19, 21, 23, 24–51
Everest, Mt. **9**, **72**, 83, 87
Eyre, L. 98, 101

F
Fairbanks 57
Falkand Is. 14, **65**, 71
Faroe Is. 25
Fès 92
Fiji **98**, 99, 104
Finland 15, **22**, 23, 25, **25**, **27**, 29, 107
Finland, Gulf of 29
Florence 41
Florida 57, **59**
Fort-de-France **53**, 63
Fort Worth 57
Fortaleza **64**, 69
France 15, **20**, **21**, **22**, 23, **24**, 25, **27**, 33
Frankfurt 57, **59**
Frankfurt am Main 37
Frankfurt an der Oder 37
Freemantle 101
Freetown **91**, 94
French Guiana 14, 65, **65**, 67
French Polynesia 99, **99**
Frisian Is. 35
Fuji, Mt. 89
Fukuoka 89

G
Gabon 15, 23, **91**, 91, 95
Gaborone **91**, 97
Gambia, The 14, 91, **91**, 94
Ganges, R. 9, 83
Garda, L. 41
Garonne, R. 33
Gascony 33
Gävle 29
Gaza 77
Gaziantep 77
Gdańsk 47
Geneva 39
Genoa **25**, 41
Georgetown **65**, 67
Georgia (US) 57, **59**
Georgia **26**, 48, **51**
Geraldton 101
Germany 15, **20**, **22**, 23, 25, **26**, 27, 37
Ghana 15, **90**, 91, 95
Ghent **24**, 35
Gibraltar 25, **26**, 43
Gibson Desert 101
Glasgow **24**, 31
Gobi 9, **9**, 87
Good Hope, Cape of 97

Gothenburg 29
Gotland 29
Grampian Mts. 31
Gran Chaco 71
Granada 43
Grand Canyon 56
Great Australian Bight 101
Great Barrier Reef 101
Great Bear L. 54, 107
Great Dividing Range 101
Great Falls 56
Great Salt L. 56
Great Sandy Desert 101
Great Slave L. 54–5, 107
Great Victoria Desert 101
Greece 15, 23, 25, **26**, 45
Greenland **9**, 14, **52**, 53, 107
Grenada **14**, 53, **53**, 63
Grenoble 33
Groningen **24**, 35
Guadalajara **52**, 61
Guadalquivir, R. 43
Guadeloupe **53**, 63
Guadiana, R. 43
Guam 99, **99**, 105
Guangzhou 87
Guatemala 14, **21**, **52**, 53, 61
Guatemala City **52**, 61
Guayaquil 67
Guernsey 31
Guinea 14, 23, **23**, 91, **91**, 94
Guinea, Gulf of 95
Guinea-Bissau 14, 91, **91**, 94
Guiyang 87
Gulf, Persian 79, 81
Guyana 14, 65, **65**, 67
Gwalior 83

H
Haarlem 35
Hague, The **24**, 35
Haifa **74**, 77
Haiti 14, 53, **53**, 63
Hakodate 89
Halifax 55
Halle 37
Hamburg **26**, 37
Hamilton (Bermuda) **53**, 63
Hamilton (Canada) 55
Hamilton (NZ) **98**, 103
Hangzhou 87
Hankow **10**, 11
Hannover 37
Hanoi **73**, 84
Harare **91**, 97
Harbin 87
Harrisburg 57, **59**
Hartford 57, **59**
Harz Mts. 37
Havana **53**, 62–3
Hawaii **8**, 56, **59**, 99
Hebrides 31
Helena 56, **59**
Helsinki **25**, 29
Hilversum 35
Himalayas (mts.) 9, **9**, 83, 86–7
Hindu Kush (mts.) 81
Hiroshima 89
Hispaniola 63
Ho Chi Minh City 84
Hobart **98**, 101
Hofuf **74**, 79
Hokkaido 89
Holland see Netherlands
Honduras 14, 53, **53**, 61
Hong Kong 15, 87
Honiara 99, 105
Honshu **9**, 89
Hormuz, Straits of 81
Horn, Cape 71
Houston **52**, 57
Huang (Yellow), R. **9**, 87
Hudson Bay 55
Hungary 15, 23, 25, **25**, 47
Huron, L. **9**, 55, 57
Hyderabad **16**, 83

I
Ibadan 95
Ibagué 67
Ibiza 43
Iceland 14, 25, **25**, 29, 107

Idaho 56, **59**
Iguaçu Falls 69
IJsselmeer 35
Illinois 57, **59**
India **14**, 15, 20, 21, 23, **23**, **72**, 73, 83
Indian Ocean 9, **9**, 95
Indiana 57, **59**
Indianapolis 57, **59**
Indonesia **14**, 15, 20, 21, 23, **23**, 72, 73, 84–5
Indus, R. 83
Innsbruck 39
Invercargill 103
Inverness 31
Ionian Sea 41, 45
Iowa 57, **59**,
Iquique 71
Iquitos 67
Iráklion 45
Iran 15, 23, **23**, 73, **74**, 75, 81
Iraq 15, 23, **23**, 73, 75, **75**, 81
Ireland 15, 25, **25**, 27, 31
Irian Jaya 85
Irish Sea 31
Irkutsk 49
Irrawaddy, R. 84
Iskenderun 77
Islamabad **72**, 83
Israel 15, 73, **74**, 75, 77
Istanbul **16**, 17, **74**, 77
Italy 15, **21**, **22**, 25, **25**, 27, 41
Izmir **74**, 77

J
Jackson 57, **59**
Jacksonville 57
Jaipur 83
Jakarta 16, 17, **72**, 84
Jamaica 14, 22, **23**, 53, **53**, 63
Japan 14, 15, 20, 22, 23, **72**, 73, 89
Japan, Sea of 89
Java 84–5
Java Sea 85
Jefferson City 57, **59**
Jerez 43
Jersey 31
Jerusalem **74**, 77
Jiddah **74**, 79
Jinan 87
Jinja 95
Johannesburg 97
Jönköping 29
Jordan 15, 73, 75, **75**, 77
Jotunheimen (mt.) 29
Juba 93
Juneau 57, **59**
Jungfrau (mt.) 39
Jura Mts. 33
Jyväskylä 29

K
K2, Mt. **9**, 83
Kabul **75**, 81
Kaduna 95
Kagoshima 89
Kalahari **9**, 97
Kalgoorlie 101
Kalimantan 85
Kaliningrad 48
Kamchatka Peninsula 49
Kampala **90**, 95
Kananga 95
Kanazawa 89
Kano 95
Kanpur 83
Kansas 57, **59**
Kansas City 57
Kara Kum 48
Karachi **16**, 17, 82
Karakoram (mts.) **9**, 83
Karlsruhe 37
Kashmir 83
Kassel 37
Kathmandu **73**, 83
Katowice 47
Kattegat 29
Kawasaki 89
Kazakhstan 15, 48, **51**, **73**, 73

Kazan 48
Keflavik 29
Kentucky 57, **59**
Kenya 15, 21, **90**, 95
Kenya, Mt. 95
Kerman 81
Khabarovsk 49
Kharkov 48
Khartoum **90**, 93
Khíos 45
Kiel 37
Kiev **27**, 48, **51**
Kigali **91**, 95
Kilimanjaro (mt.) 90, 95
Kimberley 97
Kinabalu, Mt. 85
Kingston **53**, 63
Kinshasa **90**, 95
Kiribati 99, **99**
Kirkuk 81
Kirov 81
Kiruna 29
Kisangani 95
Kisumu 95
Kitakyushu 89
Klagenfurt 39
Kobe 89
Kolkata **16**, 17, **72**, 83
Konya 77
Korea 15, 22, 23, 73, **73**, 87
Kosciusko, Mt. 101
Kraków 47
Krasnodar 48
Krasnoyarsk 49
Kuala Lumpur **73**, 84
Kuching 85
Kunlun Shan (mts.) 86–7
Kunming 87
Kuopio 29
Kuril Is. 49, 107
Kuwait 15, 23, 73, 75, **75**, 79
Kyoto 89
Kyrgyzstan 15, 48, **51**, 73, **73**
Kyushu 89
Kyzyl Kum 48

L
La Coruña 43
La Paz 10, **64**, 67
La Plata **64**, 71
La Rochelle 33
La Spezia 41
Labrador 55
Lagoda, L. **25**, 48
Lagos 95
Lahore 83
Lahti 29
Land's End 31
Lansing 57, **59**
Lanzhou 87
Lanzarote 43
Laos 15, **26**, 73, **73**, 84
Lapland 29
Laredo 57
Las Palmas 43
Las Vegas 56
Latvia 15, 25, **26**, 48, **51**
Launceston 101
Lausanne 39
Le Havre 33
Le Mans 33
Lebanon 15, 73, 75, **75**, 77
Leeds **24**, 31
Leeuwarden 35
Leeward Is. 63
Leicester 31
Leiden 35
Leipzig 37
Lena, R. 9, 49, 107
León (Mexico) **52**, 60–1
León (Spain) 43
Lérida 43
Lesotho 15, 91, **91**, 97
Lésvos 45
Leuven 35
Lhasa 87
Liberia 14, 91, **91**, 94
Libreville **91**, 95
Libya 15, 23, **90**, 91, 93
Liechtenstein **14**, 25, **26**, 39
Liège **24**, 35
Ligurian Sea 41
Lille 33

Lillehammer 29
Lilongwe **91**, 97
Lima 16, **65**, 67
Limassol 77
Limerick 31
Límnos 45
Limoges 33
Limpopo, R. 97
Linares 43
Lincoln 57, **59**
Linköping 29
Linz 39
Lisbon **25**, 43
Lithuania 15, 25, **27**, 48, **51**
Little Rock 57, **59**
Liverpool 31
Livingstone 97
Livorno 41
Ljubljana **27**, 45
Llanos 67
Lobito 97
Lofoten Is. 29
Logan, Mt. 54, 107
Loire, R. 33
Lomé **91**, 95
London (Canada) 55
London (UK) 16, 17, **24**, 31
Londonderry 31
Long Beach 56
Lorca 43
Los Angeles **52**, 56
Louisiana 57, **59**
Louisville 57
Lower Hutt 103
Luanda **91**, 97
Lübeck 37
Lublin 47
Lubumbaşi 95
Lucknow 83
Lugano 39
Lugo 43
Luleá 29
Lusaka **91**, 97
Luxembourg 15, 25, 27, **27**, 35
Luzern 39
Luzon 85
Lviv 48
Lyon **24**, 33

M
Maas, R. 35
Maastricht 35
Macao 87
Macdonnell Ranges (mts.) 101
Macedonia 15, 25, **27**, 45
Mackay 101
Mackenzie, R. **9**, 54, 107
McKinley, Mt. **54**, 57, 107
Madagascar **9**, 15, 91, **91**, 97
Madeira 92
Madison 57, **59**
Madrid **25**, 43
Madurai 83
Magdeburg 37
Magellan, Straits of 71
Maggiore, L. 41
Main, R. 37
Maine 57, **59**
Mainz 37
Majorca 43
Malabo **91**, 95
Málaga **25**, 43
Malatya 77
Malawi 15, 91, **91**, 97
Malaysia 15, 21, 23, 73, **73**, 84–5
Maldives 15, **72**, 73
Malé **72**
Mali 15, 20, 91, **91**, 92
Malmö 29
Malta **14**, 25, **26**
Man, I. of 31
Managua **52**, 61
Manama **75**
Manaus 69
Manchester 31
Manchuria 87
Mandalay 84
Manila **73**, 85
Manitoba 55
Manizales 67
Mannheim 37

110

Manukau 103
Maputo **91**, 97
Mar del Plata **64**, 71
Maracaibo, L. 67
Markham, Mt. 106
Marrakesh 92
Marseille **24**, 33
Marshall Is. 99, **99**
Martinique 53, 63
Maryland 57, **59**
Maseru **91**, 97
Mashhad **74**, 81
Massachusetts 57, **59**
Massif Central (mts.) 33
Masterton 103
Mato Grosso 69
Matterhorn (mt.) 39
Mauritania 14, 91, **91**, 92
Mauritius 15, 91, **91**, 97
Mayotte **91**, 97
Mbabane **91**, 97
Mecca **74**, 79
Mechelen 35
Medan 84
Medellín 67
Medicine Hat 55
Medina **74**, 79
Mediterranean Sea 33, 43
Mekong, R. 84, 87
Melanesia 99
Melbourne **98**, 101
Melville I. 55
Memphis 57
Mendoza **64**, 71
Menorca 43
Mérida 61
Messina 41
Metz 33
Meuse, R. *see* Maas
Mexico 14, 20, 21, 22, 23,
    52, 53, 60–1
Mexico, Gulf of 57, 61
Mexico City 16, **52**, 61
Miami 57
Michigan 57, **59**
Michigan, L. **9**, 55, 57
Micronesia, Federated
    States of 99, **99**
Middlesborough 31
Milan **25**, 41
Milwaukee 57
Mindanao 85
Minna **10**, 11
Minneapolis 57
Minnesota 57, **59**
Minsk **27**, 48, **51**
Miskolc 47
Mississippi 57, **59**
Mississippi, R. 8, **9**, **52**, 57
Missouri 57, **59**
Missouri R. 57
Modena 41
Mogadishu **91**, 93
Moldova 15, **25**, **26**, 48, **51**
Moluccas Is. 85
Mombasa 95
Monaco **14**, 25, **26**, 33
Mongolia 15, 73, **73**, 87
Monrovia **91**, 94
Mons 35
Montana 56–7, **59**
Monterrey **52**, 61
Montevideo **65**, 71
Montgomery 57, **59**
Montpelier 57, **59**
Montpellier 33
Montréal **52**, 55
Montserrat **53**, 63
Morocco 15, **90**, 91, 92
Moroni **91**, 97
Moscow **16**, 17, **26**, 48, **51**
Moselle, R. 35, 37
Mosul 81
Moulmein 84
Mount Isa 101
Mozambique 15, 91, **91**, 97
Mulhouse 33
Mumbai (Bombay) **16**, 17,
    72, 83
Munich **26**, 37
Münster 37
Murcia 43
Murmansk 48, 107
Murray, R. **98**, 101
Murrumbidgee, R. 101

Muscat **75**, 79
Mwanza 95
Myanmar (Burma) 15, 20,
    73, **73**, 84
Mysore 83

N
Nagasaki 89
Nagoya **72**, 89
Nagpur 83
Nairobi **90**, 95
Namibia 15, 23, 91, **91**, 97
Namur 35
Nanchang 87
Nancy 33
Nanda Devi (mt.) 83
Nanjing 87
Nanning 87
Nantes 33
Napier 103
Naples **25**, 41
Narvik 29
Nashville 57, **59**
Nassau **53**, 63
Nasser, L. 93
Nauru **14**, 99, **99**
Náxos 45
Ndjamena **91**, 93
Neagh, Lough 31
Nebraska 57, **59**
Neckar, R. 37
Nelson 103
Nepal 15, 73, **73**, 83
Netherlands 15, 23, **24**, 25,
    27, 35
Netherlands Antilles **53**, 63
Neuchâtel 39
Neusiedler, L. 39
Nevada 56, **59**
New Britain 105
New Brunswick 55
New Caledonia 23, 99, **99**
New Delhi **16**, 17, **72**, 83
New Hampshire 57, **59**
New Jersey 57, **59**
New Mexico 57, **59**
New Orleans 57
New Plymouth 103
New South Wales **98**, 101
New York (city) 16, **16**, **52**,
    57
New York (state) 57, **59**
New Zealand 15, **98**, 99,
    103
Newcastle (Aust.) 101
Newcastle upon Tyne 31
Newfoundland 55
Niagara Falls 57
Niamey **91**, 93
Nicaragua 14, **52**, 53, 61
Nice **24**, 33
Nicosia **26**, 77
Niger 15, **20**, 23, 91, **91**, 93
Nigeria **14**, 15, **20**, 23, **90**,
    91, 95
Niigata 89
Nijmegen 35
Nile, R. **9**, **9**, **90**, 93
Nîmes 33
Niš 45
Niue **99**
Nizhniy Novgorod (Gorkiy)
    48
Nome 57
Norfolk 57
Norfolk I. **99**
Normandy 33
Norrköping 29
North America 8, **8**, 10, 11,
    12, 14, 16, 17, 18, 19,
    20, 22, 52–59
North Cape 29
North Carolina 57, **59**
North Dakota 57, **59**
North Korea **73**, 87
North Pole 107
North Sea 31, 35, 37
North West Territories 54–
    55
Northampton 31
Northern Ireland 24, 31
Northern Marianas 99
Northern Territory **98**, 101
Norway 15, 23, 25, **25**, 29,
    107

Norwich 31
Nottingham 31
Nouakchott **91**, 92
Nova Iguaçu **64**, 69
Nova Scotia 55
Novara 41
Novaya Zemlya 49, 107
Novosibirsk 49
Nubian Desert 93
Nullarbor Plain 101
Nunavut 54–55
Nürnberg 37
Nyasa, L. 97

O
Oakland 56
Oaxaca 61
Ob, R. 9, **9**, 49, 107
Oceania 8, 11, 13, 15, 17,
    19, 21, 23, 98–105
Odense **24**, 29
Oder, R. 37
Odessa 48
Ogaden 93
Ohio 57, **59**
Okavango Swamp 97
Okhotsk, Sea of 49, 107
Oklahoma 57, **59**
Oklahoma City 57, **59**
Öland 29
Oldenburg 37
Olympia 56, **59**
Olympus, Mt. 45
Omaha 57, **59**
Oman 15, 73, 75, **75**, 79
Oman, Gulf of 79, 81
Omdurman 93
Omsk 49
Onega, L. 48
Ontario 55
Ontario, L. 55, 57
Oomaru 103
Oporto 43
Oradea 45
Oran 93
Orange, R. 97
Örebro 29
Oregon 56, **59**
Orinoco, R. 67
Orkney Is. 31
Orléans 33
Oruro 67
Osaka **72**, 89
Oslo **25**, 29
Osnabrück 37
Ostend 35
Ostrava 47
Otranto, Strait of 41
Ottawa **52**, 55
Ouagadougou **91**, 95
Oulu 29
Oviedo 43
Oxford 31

P
Pacific Ocean 8–9, **9**, 98–9,
    104–5
Padua 41
Pakistan 14, 15, 21, 22, **72**,
    73, 82–3
Palermo 41
Palma 43
Palmerston North 103
Pamirs (mts.) 48
Pampas 71
Pamplona 43
Panama 14, 53, **53**, 61
Papeete **99**, 105
Papua New Guinea 15, **98**,
    99, 105
Paraguay 14, 65, **65**, 71
Paramaribo **65**, 67
Paris **24**, 33
Parma 41
Patagonia 71
Patna 83
Pau 33
Peace, R. **9**, 54
Peloponnese 43
Pennines 31
Pennsylvania 57, **59**
Périgueux 33
Perpignan 33
Persian Gulf 79, 81
Perth **98**, 101

Peru 14, 22, 23, 65, **65**, 67
Perugia 41
Pescara 41
Peshawar 83
Petropavlovsk 48
Philadelphia **52**, 57
Philippines 15, 73, **73**, 85
Phnom Penh **73**, 84
Phoenix 56, **59**
Picardy 33
Pierre 57, **59**
Pindus Mts. 45
Piraeus 45
Pisa 41
Pitcairn Is. 99, **99**
Pittsburgh 57
Plenty, Bay of 103
Ploieşti 45
Plovdiv 45
Plymouth 31
Plzeň 47
Po, R. 41
Poitiers 33
Poland 15, 22, 23, 25, **26**, 47
Polynesia 99
Pomerania 47
Popayán 67
Port-au-Prince **53**, 63
Port Elizabeth 97
Port Hedland 101
Port Lincoln 101
Port Louis **91**
Port Moresby **98**, 105
Port Said 93
Port Stanley **65**, 71
Port Sudan 93
Pôrto Alegre 69
Porto Novo **91**, 95
Portsmouth 31
Portugal 15, 25, **25**, **27**, 43
Potsdam 37
Poznań 47
Prague **27**, 47
Pretoria **91**, 97
Prince Edward I. 55
Providence 57, **59**
Puebla **52**, 61
Puerto Montt 71
Puerto Rico 14, 53, **53**, 63
Pune 83
Punjab 83
Pyongyang **73**, 87
Pyrenees (mts.) 33, 43

Q
Qandahar 81
Qatar 15, 73, 75, **75**, 79
Qattara Depression 93
Qazvin 81
Qingdao 87
Qom 81
Québec 55
Queen Elizabeth Is. 55, 107
Queensland **98**, 101
Quetta 82
Quezon City 85
Quimper 33
Quito **64**, 67

R
Rabat **90**, 92
Rabaul 105
Radom 47
Rainier, Mt. 56
Raleigh 57, **59**
Rangoon **73**, 84
Ravenna 41
Rawalpindi 83
Reading 31
Recife 69
Red Rock, R. 9, 57
Red Sea 79
Regensburg 37
Reggio 41
Reggio di Calabria 41
Regina 55
Reims 33
Reindeer L. 55
Rennes 33
Republic of Congo 15, 91,
    91, 95
Réunion I. 15, 91, **91**, 97
Reykjavik **25**, 29, 107
Rhine, R. 37, 39

Rhode Island 57, **59**
Rhodes 45
Rhône, R. 33, 39
Richmond 57, **59**
Riga **26**, 48, 51
Rimini 41
Rio de Janeiro 16, **64**, 69
Rio Grande 57
Riyadh **74**, 79
Rocky Mts. 8, 54, 56–7, 107
Roeselare 35
Romania 15, 20, 23, 25, **27**,
    45
Rome **25**, 41
Rosa, Monte (mt.) 39, 41
Rosario **64**, 71
Roseau **53**, 63
Ross Sea 106
Rostock 37
Rostov 48
Rotorua 103
Rotterdam **24**, 35
Rouen 33
Ruapehu (mt.) 103
Rub'al Khali 79
Ruhr, R. 37
Russia 14, 15, 20, 22, 23,
    25, **26**, 80–1, **83**
Rwanda 15, 91, **91**, 95
Rzeszów 47

S
Saarbrücken 37
Sabadell 43
Sabah 85
Sacramento 56, **59**
Sahara 9, 92–3
Saint Denis **91**
St. Gotthard Pass 39
Saint John 55
St. John's 55
St. Kitts (Christopher)-Nevis
    53
St. Lawrence, R. 27, 29
St. Louis 33, 39
St. Lucia 53, **53**, 63
St. Nazaire 33
St. Paul 57, **59**
St. Petersburg 16, 17, 48
St. Pierre et Miquelon 53,
    53, 55
St. Pölten 39
St. Vincent **14**, 53, **53**, 63
St. Vincent, Cape 43
Sakhalin 49, 107
Salamanca 43
Salem 56, **59**
Salerno 41
Salt Lake City 56, **59**
Salto 71
Salvador **64**, 69
Salzburg 39
Salzgitter 37
Samara 48
Samarqand 48
Sambre, R. 35
Samoa **99**, 105
Sámos 45
Samsun 77
San Antonio 57
San Diego **52**, 56
San Francisco 56
San José **52**, 61
San Juan **53**, 63
San Luis Potosí **8**, 61
San Marino **14**, 25, **26**, 41
San Salvador **52**, 61
San Sebastián 43
Santa Cruz 67
Santa Fé (Argentina) 71
Santa Fé (US) 57, **59**
Santander 43
Santiago 16, **64**, 71
Santiago de Compostela 43
Santiago de Cuba 63
Santo Domingo **53**, 63
São Paulo 16, **64**, 69
São Tomé and Principe **91**,
    95
Saône, R. 33
Sapporo 89
Sarajevo **27**, 45
Saratov 48
Sarawak 85
Sardinia 41

111

Saskatchewan 55
Saskatoon 55
Saudi Arabia 9, 15, 23, 73, **74**, 75, 79
Sault Ste. Marie 55
Savannah 57
Schelde, R. 35
Schiedam 35
Schwerin 37
Scilly, Is. of 31
Scotland 31
Seattle 56
Segovia 43
Seine, R. 33
Selvas 69
Semarang 85
Sendai 89
Senegal 14, 91, **91**, 94
Seoul **16**, 17, **73**, 87
Setúbal 43
Severn, R. 31
Seville **25**, 43
Seychelles 15, 91, **91**
Sfax 93
Shanghai **16**, 17, 87
Shannon, R. 31
Sheffield **24**, 31
Shenyang 16, 87
Shijiazhuang 87
Shikoku 89
Shiraz **74**, 81
Siberia 9, 49
Sicily 41
Siena 41
Sierra de Gredos 43
Sierra de Guadarrama 43
Sierra Leone 14, 91, **91**, 94
Sierra Madre 60–1
Sierra Morena 43
Sierra Nevada (Spain) 43
Sierra Nevada (US) 56
Silesia 47
Simplon Pass 39
Sinai 93
Singapore **10**, 11, 15, **72**, 73, 84
Siracusa 41
Skagerrak 29
Skellefteå 29
Skopje **27**, 45
Skye, I. of 31
Slovakia 15, 23, 25, **27**, 47
Slovenia 15, 25, **27**, 45
Smolensk 48
Socotra 72, 75, 79
Sofia **27**, 45
Solomon Is. 99, **99**, 105
Somalia 15, 91, **91**, 93
Somme, R. 33
Sousse 93
South Africa 15, 23, 91, **91**, 97
South America 8, **8**, 10, 11, 12, 14, 16, 17, 18, 19, 20, 22, 64–71
South Australia **98**, 101
South Carolina 57, **59**
South China Sea 84–5
South Dakota 57, **59**
South Korea **73**, 87
South Pole 106
Southampton 31
Southern Ocean 9
Spain 15, 20, 21, 22, 23, **25**, **25**, 27, 43
Springfield (Ill.) **59**
Springfield (Mass.) 57
Sri Lanka 15, 21, **72**, 73, 83
Srinagar 83
Stavanger 29
Stockholm **25**, 29
Stoke-on-Trent 31
Stralsund 31
Strasbourg **24**, 33
Stuttgart 37
Subotica 45
Sucre **64**, 67
Sudan **14**, 15, 20, **90**, 91, 93
Sudbury 55
Suez 93
Sulawesi (Celebes) 85
Sumatra 9, 84
Sundsvall 29
Superior, L. **9**, **52**, 55, 57

Surabaya 85
Sûre, R. 35
Surinam 14, 22, 65, **65**, 67
Suva **98**, 104
Swansea 31
Swaziland 15, 91, **91**, 97
Sweden 15, 22, 23, 25, **25**, 27, 29, 107
Switzerland 15, 25, **27**, 39
Sydney **98**, 101
Syria 15, **75**, **75**, 77
Szczecin 47
Szeged 47

T
Tabriz **74**, 81
Tagus, R. 43
Tahiti and Mooréa (Is.) 105
Ta'if **74**, 79
Taipei **73**, 87
Taiwan 15, 73, **73**, 87
Taiyuan 87
Tajikistan 15, 48, **51**, 73, **73**
Takamatsu 89
Takapuna 103
Tallahassee 57, **59**
Tallinn **26**, 48, **51**
Tamanrasset 93
Tampere 29
Tanganyika, L. **9**, 95
Tangier 92
Tanzania 15, 91, **91**, 95
Taranto 41
Tarawa **99**
Tarragona 43
Tasmania **98**, 101
Tatra Mts. 47
Tauranga 103
T'bilisi **26**, 48, 51
Tegucigalpa **53**, 61
Tehran **16**, 17, **74**, 81
Tel Aviv-Yafo **74**, 77
Tenerife 43
Tennessee 57, **59**
Terni 41
Terschelling 35
Texas 57, **59**
Texel 35
Thailand 15, **21**, 23, 73, **73**, 84
Thames, R. 31
Thar Desert 83
Thessaloniki 45
Thimphu **72**, 83
Thunder Bay 55
Thuringian Forest 37
Tianjin **16**, 17, 87
Tiber, R. 41
Tibet 87
Tien Shan (mts.) 86–7
Tierra del Fuego 71
Tigris, R. 77, 81
Tijuana 60
Tilburg 35
Timaru 103
Timișoara 45
Timor 85
Timor Sea 101
Tiranë **27**, 45
Tirol 39
Titicaca, L. **64**, 67
Toledo 43
Tombouctou 92
Tomsk 49
Tonga 99, **99**
Toowoomba 101
Topeka 57, **59**
Toronto **52**, 55
Torreón **52**, 61
Toshkent 48, **51**
Toulon 33
Toulouse **24**, 33
Tours 33
Townsville 101
Trabzon 77
Transylvanian Alps (mts.) 45
Trent, R. 31
Trenton 57, **59**
Trieste 41
Trinidad and Tobago 14, 53, **53**, 63
Tripoli (Lebanon) 77

Tripoli (Libya) **90**, 93
Trois Rivières 55
Tromsø 29
Trondheim 29
Troyes 33
Trujillo **65**, 67
Tucson 56
Tucumán **64**, 71
Tula 48
Tunis **91**, 93
Tunisia 15, **91**, 93
Turin **25**, 41
Turkey 15, 20, 21, 23, 25, 73, **74**, 75, 77
Turkmenistan 15, 48, **51**, 73, **73**
Turks Is. **53**, 63
Turku 29
Tuvalu **14**, 99, **99**
Tyrrhenian Sea 41

U
Udine 41
Uganda 15, 21, **90**, 91, 95
Ukraine 15, 25, **27**, 48, **51**
Ulan Bator **73**, 87
Ulan-Ude 49
Umeå 29
United Arab Emirates 15, 73, 75, **75**, 79
United Kingdom 9, 15, 20, 22, 23, **24**, 25, 27, 31
United States of America 14, 20, 21, 22, 23, **52**, 53, 56–59
Ural Mts. 48–9, 107
Uruguay 14, 65, **65**, 71
Ürümqi 87
Utah 56, **59**
Utrecht **24**, 35
Uzbekistan 15, 49, **51**, 73, **73**

V
Vaasa 29
Valdivia 71
Valence 33
Valencia (Spain) **25**, 43
Valencia (Venezuela) 67
Valladolid 43
Valparaíso 71
Van, L. 77
Vancouver **52**, 54
Vänern, L. 29
Vanua Levu 104
Vanuatu 99, **99**
Varansi 83
Varna 45
Vasteras 29

Vatican City **14**, **26**, 41
Vättern, L. 29
Venezuela 14, 22, 23, 65, **65**, 67
Venice 41
Vermont 57, **59**
Verona 41
Vesuvius (mt.) 41
Vicenza 41
Victoria (Aust.) **98**, 101
Victoria (Canada) 54
Victoria (Seychelles) **91**
Victoria I. 55, 107
Victoria Falls 97
Victoria, L. **9**, **90**, 95
Victoria, Mt. 105
Vienna **26**, 39
Vientiane **73**, 84
Vietnam 20, 73, **73**, 84–5
Vigo 43
Villach 39
Vilnius **27**, 48, **51**
Vinson Massif (mts.) 106
Virgin Is. **53**, 63
Virginia 57, **59**
Vistula, R. 47
Viti Levu 104
Vitoria 43
Vladivostock 49
Vlissingen 35
Volga, R. **9**, **25**, 48
Volgograd 48
Volta, L. 95
Vorkuta 49
Voronezh 48
Vosges 33

W
Waddenzee 35
Wagga Wagga 101
Wales 31
Wallis and Futuna Is. 99, **99**
Wanganui 103
Warsaw **26**, 47
Washington 56, **59**
Washington D.C. **52**, 57
Waterford 31
Weddell Sea 106
Wellington **98**, 103
West Virginia 57, **59**
Western Australia **98**, 101
Western Sahara 14, 91, **91**, 92
White Sea 48
Whitehorse 54
Whitney, Mt. 56
Whyalla 101
Wiesbaden 37

Wight, I. of 31
Wilhelm Mt. **98**, 105
Wilhelmshaven 37
Willemstad 53
Windhoek **91**, 97
Windward Is. 63
Winnipeg 55
Winnipeg, L. 55
Wisconsin 57, **59**
Wolverhampton 31
Wroclaw 47
Wuhan 87
Würzburg 37
Wyoming 56–7, **59**

X
Xi'an 87
Xining 87

Y
Yakutsk 49
Yangtze (Chang), R. **9**, **72**, 87
Yaoundé **90**, 95
Yazd 81
Yekaterinburg 48
Yellow Sea 87
Yellowstone National Park 56–7
Yemen 15, 73, 75, **75**, 79
Yenisei 49, 107
Yerevan **26**, 48, **51**
Yinchuan 87
Yokohama 89
Yonne, R. 33
York 31
Yucatán (peninsula) 61
Yugoslavia 15, 23, 25, **27**, 45
Yukon Territory 54

Z
Zagreb **27**, 45
Zambezi, R. 97
Zambia 15, 23, 91, **91**, 97
Zanzibar 95
Zaragoza **25**, 43
Zhanjiang 87
Zhengzhou 87
Zimbabwe 15, 23, 91, **91**, 97
Zürich 39
Zwolle 35

Acknowledgements

The publishers would like to thank the following for the use of their pictures:
ZEFA Picture Library is indicated as **Z** throughout
Tony Stone Images is indicated as **TSI** throughout
Robert Harding Picture Library is indicated as **RHPL** throughout
Page 1 TSI/S. & N. Geary; p3 TSI; p24 TSI/R. Passmore; p26 Z/Strachil; p27 TSI/N. Beer; p28 *left* Z/Edel *top right* Z/Damm *bottom right* Danish Dairy Board; p29 Z/Eugen; p30 *left* TSI/D. Higgs *right* TSI; p31 TSI; p32 *left* /RHPL/R. Curdy *right* TSI/C. Kempf ; p33 *top* French Railways *bottom* Magnum/Zachmann; p34 *left* Z/Streichen *right* TSI/J. Yates; p35 Netherlands Board of Tourism; p36 *left* TSI/R. Everts *right* Z/Deuter; p37 Carla Arnold; p38 *left* Z/R. Nicolas *right* TSI/M. Mehlig; p40 *left* Fiat *right* Hutchison Library; p41 TSI/M. Mehlig; p42 *left* TSI/S. Johnson *right* TSI/O. Benn; p43 Magnum/ S. Franklin; p44 *left* TSI/R.Everts *right* TSI/M. Caldwell; p45 *top* Z/Dr. H. Kramarz *bottom* Z; p46 *left* TSI/R. Everts *right* Z; p47 Magnum/E. Erwitt; p48 Frank Spooner Pictures/V. Shone; p49 Z; p50 *top* Linda Proud *middle* Z *bottom* Novosti; p51 Z; p52 TSI/J. Kopee; p54 *top* Z/Hunter *bottom* Z/K. Kummels; p55 TSI; p56 TSI/D. Schultz; p57 TSI; p58 *top* TSI/M. Segal *middle* Z/Stefnmans *bottom* RHPL/G. & P. Lorrigan; p59 TSI/M. Brooke; p60 Z; p61 *left* TSI/G. Prentice *right* RHPL/G. & P. Lorrigan; p62 Hutchison Library/P. Wolmuth; p63 *top* RHPL *bottom* TSI/W. Rudolph; p64 TSI/P. Gittoes; p65 Z; p66 TSI; p67 Z; p68 *left* Art Directors *top right* TSI/S. Cunningham *bottom right* Z/J. Heydecker; p70 *left* TSI/D. Levy *right* Hutchison Library; p71 *top* TSI/D. Levy *bottom* TSI/T. Zimmerman; p72 TSI; p74 *top* Z/Maroon *bottom* Z; p76 *left* Mepha/Jill Brown *right* Sonia Halliday; p77 *top* Z *bottom* TSI; p78 *left* Planet Earth Pictures/H.C. Heap *right* Z; p79 TSI; p80 *left* RHPL *right* Z/K.Schulz; p81 *top* TSI *bottom* RHPL; p82 *left* A. Smith *right* Z/H. Raze; p83 Z/Sunak; p84 RHPL; p85 TSI; p86 *top* TSI/A. le Garsmeur *bottom* TSI/Osmond; p87 Hutchison Picture Library; p88 *left* Photo Original *right*, TSI; p89 *top* Hutchison Picture Library *bottom* TSI; p90 Frank Spooner Pictures; p92 Z; p93 *left* Frank Spooner Pictures/M. Deville *right* Hutchison Picture Library; p94 *left* Hutchison Picture Library *right* Z/E. Earp; p95 TSI/I.; p96 *left* TSI/I. Murphy *right* RHPL/C. Jopp; p97 Hutchison Picture Library; p100 *left* TSI/S. & N. Geary *right* TSI; p101 TSI; p102 TSI/R. Smith; p103 TSI; p104 Z/E. Christian; p105 RHPL; p106 RHPL/G. Renner; p107 RHPL/W. Herbert. Picture research by Linda Proud

Every effort has been made to contact copyright holders of any material reproduced throughout this book. Any omissions will be rectified in subsequent printings if notice is given to the publisher.